Economic Boom or Ecologic Doom?

DIRECTIONS IN DEVELOPMENT
Infrastructure

Economic Boom or Ecologic Doom?

Using Spatial Analysis to Reconcile Road Development with Forest Conservation

Alvaro Federico Barra, Mathilde Burnouf, Richard Damania, and Jason Russ

WORLD BANK GROUP

ISBN (paper): 978-1-4648-0810-4
ISBN (electronic): 978-1-4648-0811-1
DOI: 10.1596/978-1-4648-0810-4

Cover photo: An aerial view of Masisi Territory in the North Kivu province of the Democratic Republic of Congo. © UN Photo/Marie Frechon. Used with the permission of UN Photo/Marie Frechon. Further permission required for reuse.
Cover design: Debra Naylor, Naylor Design, Inc.

Library of Congress Cataloging-in-Publication Data
Names: Damania, Richard, editor. | World Bank, issuing body.
Title: Economic Boom or Ecologic Doom? : Using Spatial Analysis to Reconcile Road Development with Forest Conservation / World Bank.
Description: Washington, DC : World Bank, 2016. | "This report was prepared by a team led by Richard Damania comprising (in alphabetical order) Alvaro Federico Barra, Mathilde Burnouf and Jason Daniel Russ."
Identifiers: LCCN 2016013764 (print) | LCCN 2016017181 (ebook) | ISBN 9781464808104 (pdf) | ISBN 9781464808111 | ISBN 9781464808111 ()
Subjects: LCSH: Transportation and state—Congo (Democratic Republic) | Economic development—Congo (Democratic Republic) | Deforestation—Congo (Democratic Republic)
Classification: LCC HE285.5 .T73 2016 (print) | LCC HE285.5 (ebook) | DDC 388/.049096751—dc23
LC record available at https://lccn.loc.gov/2016013764

Contents

Boxes

Figures

Maps

Tables

Foreword

Roads are vital for poverty alleviation and development. They are the arteries that connect goods to markets, workers to jobs, and children to schools. However, roads can have unintended consequences and are often the precursors to deforestation. Opening up access to a region not only allows wealth and commerce to flow in but also enables resources to be extracted and flow out. With new roads, loggers, whether legally sanctioned or not, can more easily access forests for timber; opportunities emerge to claim forested land in search of wealth; and new inhabitants are able to fell trees for firewood.

These issues are especially important in the Democratic Republic of Congo (DRC), which is the focus of this report. Decades of conflict have left the DRC with transport infrastructure that is inadequate to spur development. The country has one of the lowest road densities in the world, and most of the country's provincial capitals are unconnected to Kinshasa, the capital city.

At the same time, the DRC is home to the world's second-largest rain forest after the Amazon. The carbon sequestered by these forests corresponds to about three to five years of carbon dioxide equivalent emitted globally. The forests are also an important source of livelihood and income for the rural poor. Biodiversity in these forests is of global significance, with a disproportionately high number of species that are unique to the region—but also endangered. Degrading the country's forests would cause severe ecological impacts with local and global economic consequences.

Conventional attempts to resolve the familiar tension between conservation imperatives and development needs have relied on mitigation of damage to the environment through engineering solutions and a variety of other safeguards. Although useful and pragmatic, this approach has limits, especially when infrastructure is built in environmentally fragile areas.

This report introduces a proactive approach that emphasizes the need to consider impacts at the very outset of the planning process. It develops innovative techniques that allow decision makers to steer development away from ecological hotspots toward areas where benefits can be maximized and adverse impacts avoided.

Using cutting-edge techniques and drawing on a variety of disciplines—including spatial analysis, econometrics, and biology—this report establishes a new methodology for predicting, at fine spatial scales, the benefits that infrastructure will bring to local populations, as well as the effects that it will have on forested areas. It also develops a novel metric of biodiversity to identify regions where flora and fauna are most sensitive and where their protection is most important. These tools offer a standardized and scientific way of assessing the environmental risks of an infrastructure investment while also offering alternatives that may be equally beneficial, but less risky. The approach developed in this report will allow decision makers to tailor investments to maximize economic benefits while avoiding ecological damage.

Balancing economic growth with environmental protection is a challenge faced by nearly every nation on Earth. This report makes an important contribution to this effort that will enhance the ability of governments, donors, and policy makers to make better informed and more effective decisions.

Laura Tuck
Vice President, Sustainable Development
The World Bank

Acknowledgments

This report was prepared by a team led by Richard Damania and comprising Alvaro Federico Barra, Mathilde Burnouf, and Jason Daniel Russ.

The strategic support of Ahmadou Moustapha Ndiaye (Country Director, the Democratic Republic of Congo) and Yisgedullish Amde (Country Program Coordinator, the Democratic Republic of Congo) are gratefully acknowledged. The team is also grateful to Benoit Bosquet (Practice Manager, Environment and Natural Resources, World Bank) for his guidance and advice. Special gratitude is due to Jean Christophe Carret (Sector Leader, the Democratic Republic of Congo) for his encouragement and assistance at every stage of this report's development, including as a peer reviewer. The support of Mohammed Dalil Essakali (Senior Infrastructure Economist, Transport and ICT [Information and Communication Technology], World Bank) for advice, support, and help in data gathering and as a reviewer is also acknowledged. Nagaraja Rao Harshadeep (Harsh) (Global Lead, Watersheds, Environment and Natural Resources, World Bank) provided extremely helpful comments and assistance.

During preparation of this report, several agencies of the government of the Democratic Republic of Congo provided incisive comments and support. Notable are the contributions of the Prime Minister's Economic Council, the Infrastructure Unit, Sustainable Development MECNT (Ministry of Environment, Nature Conservation and Tourism), Cellular Infrastructure, and National REDD (Reducing Emissions from Deforestation and Forest Degradation) Coordination.

The Food and Agriculture Organization, Directorate of Forest Inventory and Planning, U.S. Agency for International Development, African Wildlife Foundation, Wildlife Conservation Society, World Resource Institute, Observatoire Satellitale des Forêts d'Afrique Centrale, and World Wildlife Fund, as well as stakeholders from the University of Kinshasa, ERAIFT (Ecole Régionale post-universitaire d'Aménagement et de gestion Intégrés des Forêts et Territoires tropicaux), all provided advice and comments on earlier versions of the study.

Note that in 2006, the government of the Democratic Republic of Congo adopted a new constitution that mandated its 11 provinces be further divided into 26 provinces. At the time of publication, this plan was still being implemented. Therefore, the data used in this analysis precede the change, and provinces referenced herein are based on the original 11 provinces.

About the Authors

Alvaro Federico Barra is a land administration/geospatial specialist at the World Bank. Since joining the World Bank in 2008, he has been involved in numerous geospatial/economics knowledge and analytical products for the Africa Region, where he has applied these innovative techniques in several sectors, including infrastructure; urban, rural, and social development; environment; and agriculture. Before joining the World Bank, he worked as a consultant at the Consultative Group to Assist the Poor (CGAP), Winrock International, and the U.N. Economic Commission for Latin America and the Caribbean. He holds a bachelor's degree in economics from Universidad Nacional de Córdoba (Argentina) and an MS in public policy and management from Carnegie Mellon University.

Mathilde Burnouf is a communications consultant in the field of international cooperation and advocacy, with more than eight years of experience as a communications consultant all over the world, but especially in Africa and Southeast Asia. She has a proven track record in the creation and implementation of global communications strategies pertaining to international development and natural resource management. She has a master's (with honors) degree in globalization and international economic law from Sciences Politiques, Paris, and a master's degree in international affairs from University Paris 1–Sorbonne, Paris.

Richard Damania is the global lead economist in the World Bank's Water Practice. Prior to this position he was the lead economist of the Africa Sustainable Development Department, with responsibility for infrastructure, environment, and social issues. He has also served as lead economist in the South Asia and Latin America and Caribbean Regions of the World Bank. Before joining the World Bank, he was at the University of Adelaide in Australia. He has held numerous advisory positions in government and international organizations and serves on the editorial board of several academic journals in natural resource economics. He has an MA and a PhD in economics, both from the University of Glasgow.

Jason Russ is an economist in the World Bank's Water Practice. Since joining the Bank in 2012, he has been working on research related to the fields of sustainable development, transport economics, and the economics of water. Prior to joining the World Bank, he was a consultant at PricewaterhouseCoopers. He earned a BA from the University of Maryland, College Park; an MA in economics from Fordham University; and is currently a candidate for a PhD in economics at George Washington University.

Executive Summary

Motivation

The natural endowment of the Democratic Republic of Congo, in the form of land, minerals, and forests, is unparalleled. The right mix of policies could potentially unleash incentives that could transform the economy perhaps even to middle-income status. The agricultural sector generates about 40 percent of total income and employs 60 percent of the workforce. Mining accounts for 12 percent of gross domestic product (GDP); some estimates put the Democratic Republic of Congo's mineral wealth at US$24 trillion. Perhaps the country's best-known natural asset is its vast forest estate. Home to more than 145 million hectares of rain forests, the Democratic Republic of Congo has the second-largest forest endowment in the world, and contains more than 60 percent of the total forest area in the Congo Basin. These forests are of global importance in that they represent the second-largest carbon sink in the world and have considerable potential to generate income for the Democratic Republic of Congo through the Reducing Emissions from Deforestation and Forest Degradation (REDD+) mechanism. Locally, too, forests are of paramount importance. Up to 40 percent of individuals living in the country's forested provinces rely on hunting, forest products, and fishing as their main sources of food (De Merode, Homewood, and Cowlishaw 2003).

However, GDP (wealth) in the Democratic Republic of Congo is geographically concentrated. Map ES.1 illustrates that aside from the area around Kinshasa, the capital, significant peaks in income can be seen around Lubumbashi, the country's mining capital, which has enormous deposits of copper and cobalt; Mbuji-Mayi, an area rich in diamonds; and Kivu, which has large deposits of gold and other rare-earth metals.

Given the vast distances and extreme variations in the spatial distribution of GDP, connecting regions that flourish with those that lag could provide a significant boost to economic growth. There is thus an urgent need for improving both interprovincial and intraprovincial connectivity to promote trade and economic cohesion.

The objective of this report is to present new tools for prioritizing infrastructure investments and guiding their location. It recognizes that investment needs far outstrip available resources, so needs must be prioritized and impacts objectively quantified. Accordingly, the report illustrates techniques for identifying the

Map ES.1 Local GDP in the Democratic Republic of Congo, 2006

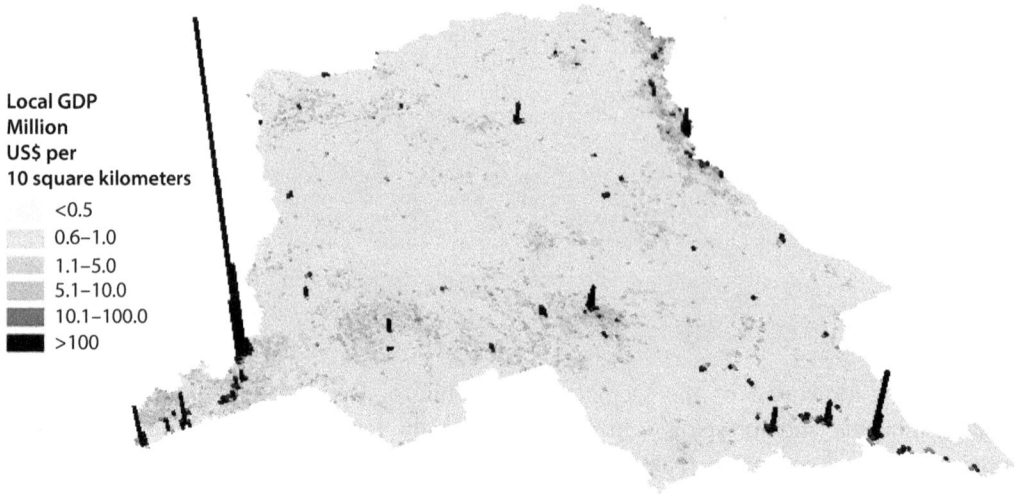

Local GDP
Million
US$ per
10 square kilometers

- <0.5
- 0.6–1.0
- 1.1–5.0
- 5.1–10.0
- 10.1–100.0
- >100

Source: Ghosh and others 2010.
Note: GDP = gross domestic product.

benefits of investment at a highly disaggregated spatial scale and recognizes that certain costs and externalities also need to be considered, especially in the Democratic Republic of Congo. The approach is illustrated in the context of transport infrastructure, but can also be applied with modifications to other sectoral investments.

Transport infrastructure in the Democratic Republic of Congo is among the sparsest and most dilapidated in the world (map ES.2). In many parts of the country, traveling to the capital, Kinshasa, by road is impossible and many of the provincial capitals are unconnected to Kinshasa. Despite having one of the largest river networks in the world, river transport is often hampered by high levels of silting and long wait times at ports because of poor infrastructure and uneven governance.

Although roads and infrastructure confer many benefits and are necessary for development, they also generate externalities and impose costs—environmental, social, and economic—that need to be considered to maximize welfare. Roads often catalyze a process of deforestation and land conversion, which means that projects must be planned and procedures established to minimize the risks of deforestation to preserve the potential revenues that could be earned by the Reducing Emissions from Deforestation and Forest Degradation (REDD+) and other initiatives. Other less recognized, localized economic costs may also emerge as roads encourage growth in areas of high economic potential at the cost of areas with a competitive and comparative disadvantage. Such spatial sorting is an inevitable and necessary consequence of economic transition based on promoting spatial productive efficiency.

Map ES.2 Diagrammatic Map of Transport in the Democratic Republic of Congo

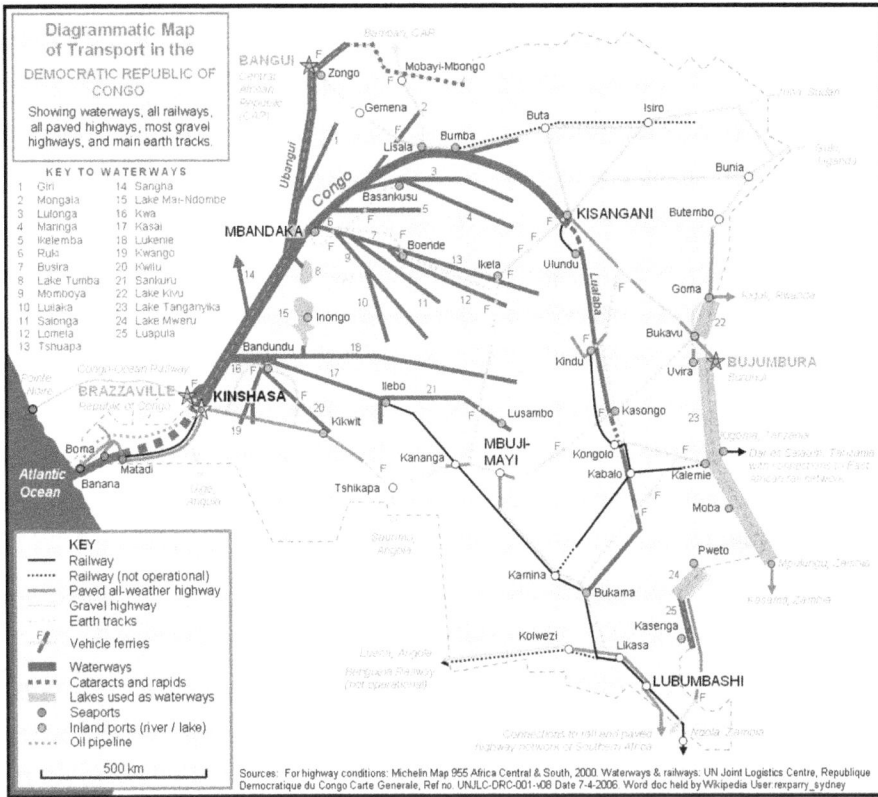

Approach

Infrastructure investments in long-lived assets, such as roads, have the ability to shape the development potential of the Democratic Republic of Congo for generations to come. This possible future suggests the need for careful planning and holistic decision-making tools that take into account the wide range of direct and induced impacts that might come about to maximize the full range of net benefits from these costly investments. This report therefore presents new information and tools that can be used by policy makers for broad planning purposes to determine where investments yield the highest net returns and how damage to valuable natural assets could be avoided.

This work considerably advances the information that is available to planners and provides methodologies that could be used to make more informed decisions to identify trade-offs and maximize net welfare benefits. The approach draws from the state of the art across a variety of disciplines—spatial geographic information system (GIS) analysis, spatial econometrics, economic theory, and conservation biology—to create an approach and set of tools that can guide the location and level of investments by estimating benefits and environmental costs at a highly disaggregated spatial scale.

Economic Boom or Ecologic Doom? • http://dx.doi.org/10.1596/978-1-4648-0810-4

The analysis proceeds in four related phases that combine economic assessments with geospatial analysis. First, transport costs are estimated using GIS techniques. A variety of econometric procedures are then used to determine the economic effects of changing transport costs to the cheapest market. The estimated elasticity measure provides a broad indication of the benefits that would accrue in each location by reducing transport costs. Second, highly disaggregated spatial data are used to estimate the effects of roads on forest cover. A novel metric of biodiversity is also developed to identify forests of high (and low) value, recognizing that not all forests have identical ecological significance. Third, the two spatial estimates are combined to simulate the effects of different policies. Finally, this report provides a series of maps that identify hotspots where risks from transport investments are high and benefits relatively low, regions where risks are low and benefits high, and regions where there are large trade-offs between economic and ecological goals.

Costs of Travel

In the first stage, a geospatial model is developed that identifies costs of and bottlenecks to travel. The model simulates how individuals and traded goods are moved. The Congolese transport system is intrinsically multimodal, with the Congo River as its spine. Panel a of map ES.3 shows the costs of transporting goods to the cheapest market from every location within the Democratic Republic of Congo (a market is defined as a city of at least 50,000 residents), using a multimodal model with access to both roads and rivers.

Panel b of map ES.3 shows the difference in costs between a unimodal model with only roads, and the multimodal model with land and river transport included. It thus shows the areas that are most likely to use and benefit from using the river for transport to reach the nearest market.

Panel b of map ES.3 shows the changes in travel costs when using rivers. It is clear from the map that, aside from some isolated areas in the northwest part of the country, rivers are used relatively infrequently for local transport. Specifically, 14 percent of individuals in the Democratic Republic of Congo live in areas where it would be cost-effective to use river transport for any portion of their trip to the local market. Furthermore, these individuals live in areas that account for only about 7 percent of the country's GDP, implying that investments in river transport will not have a significant impact on *local market* transport, given the current economic geography of the country. The implication is that the road network is likely much more cost-effective for *shorter distance local transport*. This is a well-established result and reflects the fact that river transport is typically most economic for low-value, high-volume goods that need to be transported over longer distances.

However, when Kinshasa is the desired destination, approximately 80 percent of the country's population would prefer to use river travel, at least in part (map ES.4). These individuals live in areas that account for nearly 60 percent of the country's GDP. The northern part of the country is particularly dependent on river transport for reaching Kinshasa, which is not surprising considering that much of this region has no direct road access to Kinshasa.

Map ES.3   Transport Cost to the Cheapest Market

a. Cost of transporting goods to the nearest market using a multimodal system

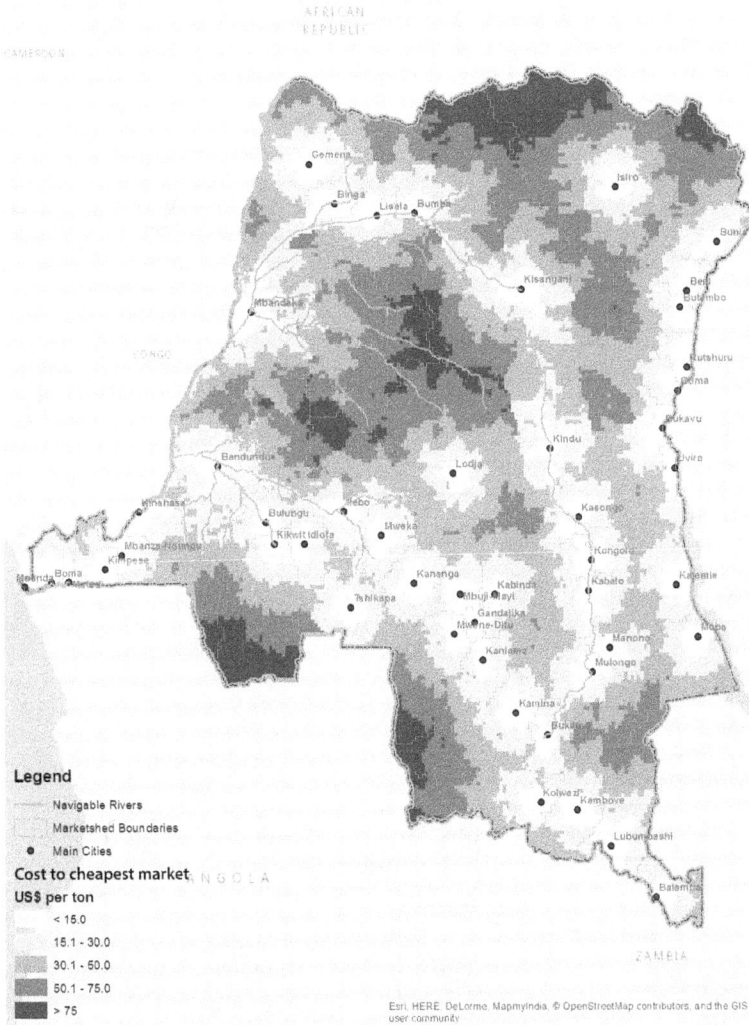

Legend

‒ Navigable Rivers

  Marketshed Boundaries

● Main Cities

Cost to cheapest market
US$ per ton

  < 15.0

  15.1 - 30.0

  30.1 - 50.0

  50.1 - 75.0

  > 75

Esri, HERE, DeLorme, MapmyIndia, © OpenStreetMap contributors, and the GIS user community

map continues next page

Economic Boom or Ecologic Doom? • http://dx.doi.org/10.1596/978-1-4648-0810-4

Map ES.3 Transport Cost to the Cheapest Market *(continued)*

b. The difference in transportation costs to the cheapest
market between a unimodal and multimodal system

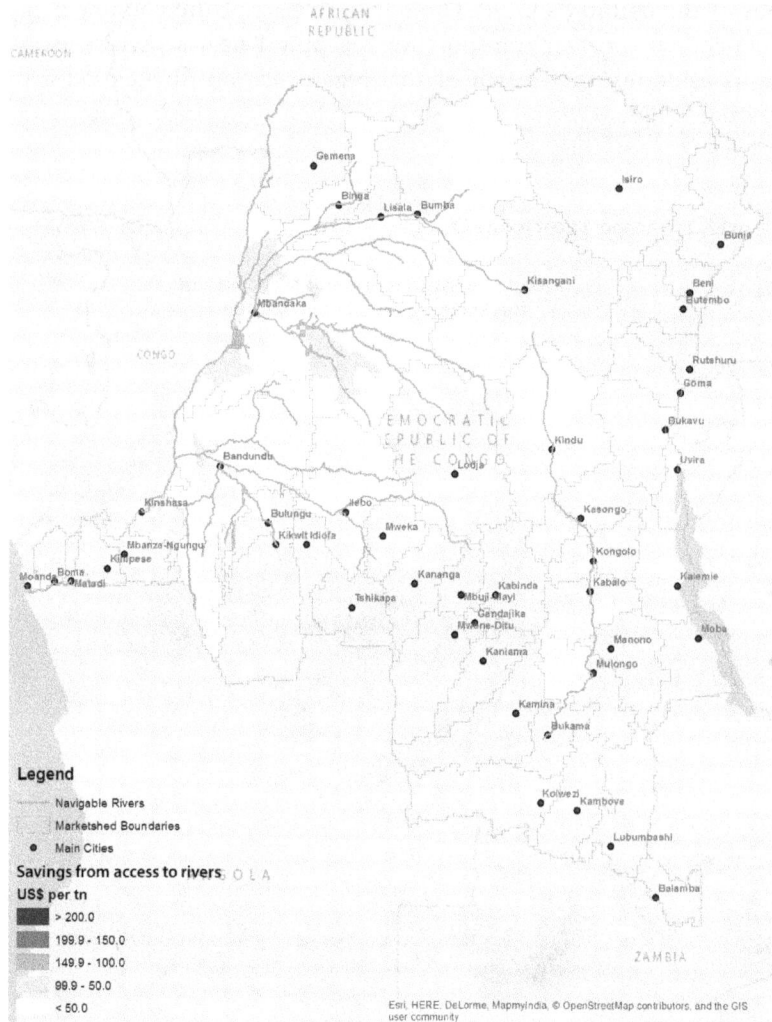

Economic Benefits

Having estimated transport costs from each location, the report uses state-of-the-art econometric methods to determine the economic effects of reducing local transport costs.[1] The results suggest that decreasing local transport costs would yield significant benefits, especially in the highest-cost, more densely populated regions. Specifically, a 10 percent reduction in local transport costs would lead to, on average, a 0.46 percent increase in local GDP. A related paper (Ali and others 2015) shows that reducing transport costs in the Democratic Republic of Congo could have a significant, positive impact on wealth accumulation and poverty reduction.

Map ES.4 The Difference in Transportation Costs to Kinshasa between a Unimodal and Multimodal System

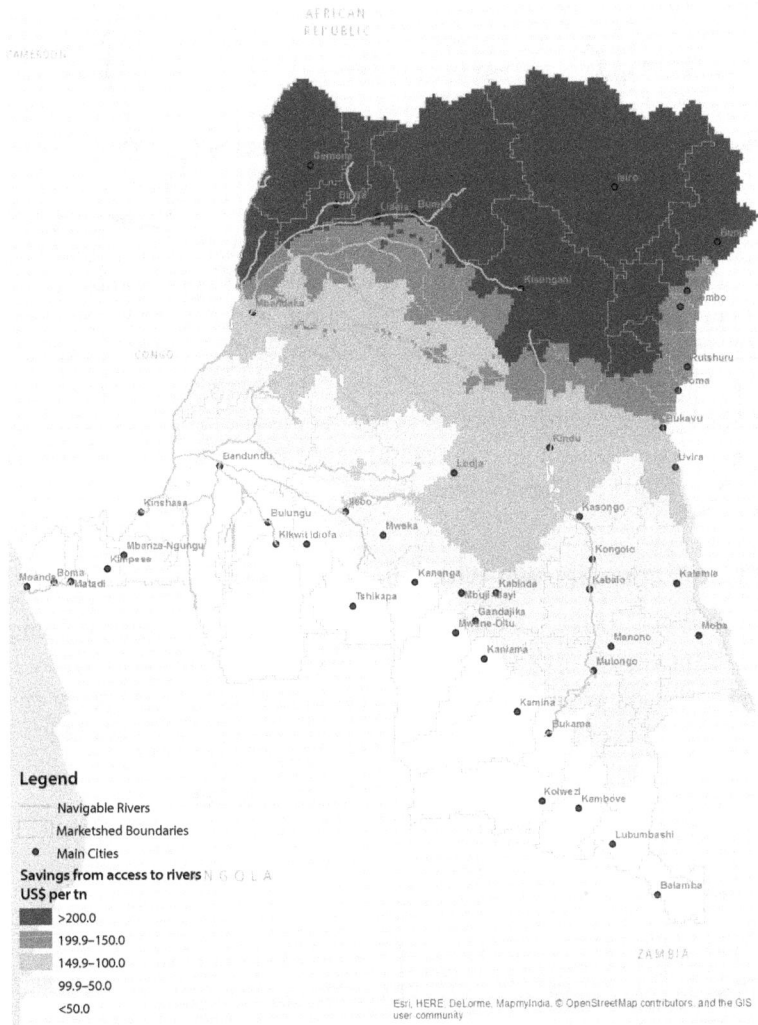

Legend

Navigable Rivers
Marketshed Boundaries
• Main Cities
**Savings from access to rivers
US$ per tn**

- >200.0
- 199.9–150.0
- 149.9–100.0
- 99.9–50.0
- <50.0

Esri, HERE, DeLorme, MapmyIndia, © OpenStreetMap contributors, and the GIS user community

Ecological Implications

In the next step, the report examines changes in forest cover induced by roads. The estimates indicate significant effects of road upgrading on the intensity and extent of forest clearing in well-defined corridors. Predicted effects of deforestation around improved road corridors vary widely with previous road conditions and locational economics, but increases in deforestation of 10–20 percent are typical.

Two patterns are noteworthy (see figure ES.1). First, upgrading roads from very poor to good condition produces near-complete deforestation within a narrow corridor (of about 1–1.5 kilometer radius) straddling the road. Second, the impact is nonlinear, and deforestation intensity falls very rapidly as distance from the road increases. Most of the deforestation occurs within about a 2 kilometer radius of the road as shown in figure ES.1. This is a useful result for planning the location of roads and suggests that small changes to location could have significant environmental benefits.

Since all forest land is of neither uniform ecological nor economic value, the report also develops a novel metric to identify areas that are of high ecological value and at higher risk of degradation. A high-resolution map of ecological vulnerability is developed that combines information on species as well as ecosystems, including measures of geographic vulnerability, extinction risk, and other aspects of the ecosystem captured through a measure of biomes developed by the World Wildlife Fund. Map ES.5 ranks regions from the most important (red) to least significant (blue) based on a composite index of desirable properties. Overall, the results suggest that at the very outset of the planning process, infrastructure siting needs to take into account effects on deforestation and biodiversity loss. The report also presents analysis that clearly shows that sequential decision making, wherein location decisions are made first, followed by an environmental impact assessment, can lead to economically less favorable outcomes that can be avoided through careful upstream planning.

Identifying Trade-Offs, Win-Wins, and Low Impacts

The report demonstrates how these results could be used to guide planning decisions. It is instructive to begin by visualizing the spatial distribution of the economy and ecology of the Democratic Republic of Congo. To do this, the

Figure ES.1 Effect of Road Quality on Forest Clearing Intensity

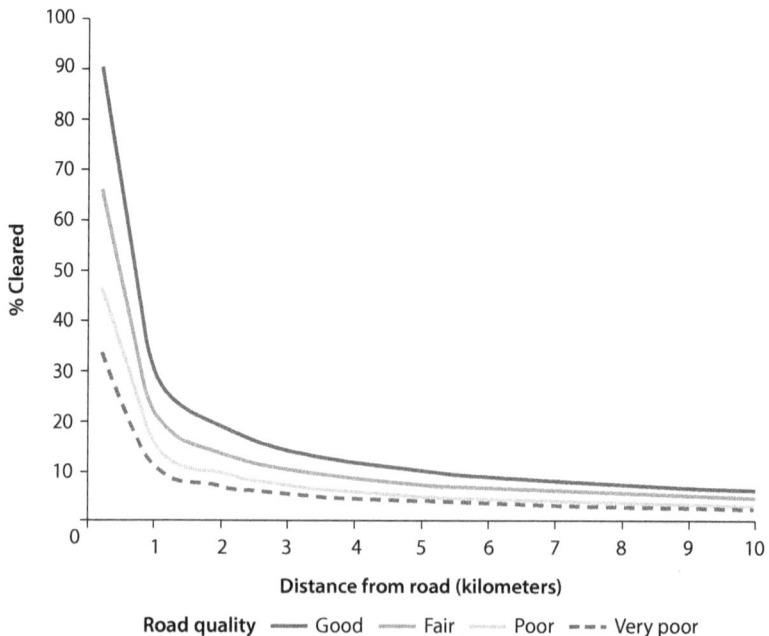

Road quality ——— Good   ——— Fair   ······ Poor   - - - Very poor

Map ES.5 Composite Species-Ecoregion Index, Congo Basin Countries

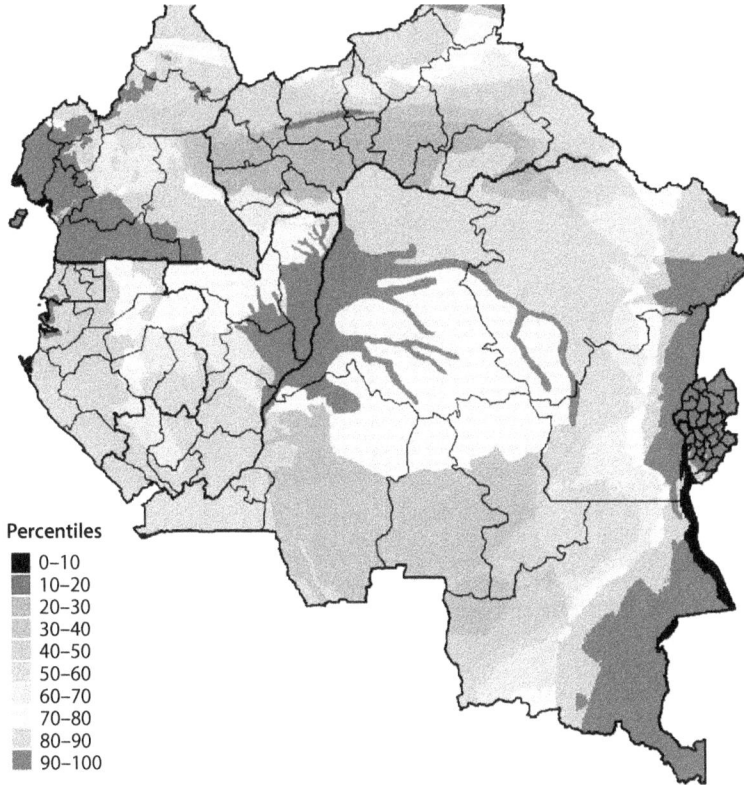

Percentiles
- 0–10
- 10–20
- 20–30
- 30–40
- 40–50
- 50–60
- 60–70
- 70–80
- 80–90
- 90–100

intersection of local GDP and the composite species-ecoregion index are shown in a combined map (map ES.6). The results suggest that quite often, the regions of the country that are most important economically also tend to contain the highest levels of sensitive biodiversity (dark blue and dark brown in map ES.6). The most important ecological areas according to the index are along the country's eastern and southeastern borders, the Congo River and its tributaries, and much of the provinces of Bas Congo and Kinshasa. These areas also tend to have higher population density and greater economic activity, with the notable exception of much of the eastern portion of Katanga province. Any development plan in these areas would impose significant risks, suggesting the need for effective policies and safeguards. However, map ES.6 also shows zones with high GDP and low ecological endowments (light blue) and vice versa (light orange). The obvious implication is that careful planning and proactive approaches can avoid sensitive areas, prioritize areas where conservation management is most needed, and encourage accelerated construction elsewhere.

How might these results be used as a practical guide to decision making? As an illustration, the report presents simulations of the potential welfare benefits, as well as deforestation, that would result from the completion of proposed road investment projects connecting major urban centers to Kinshasa using

Map ES.6 The Economy and Ecology of the Democratic Republic of Congo

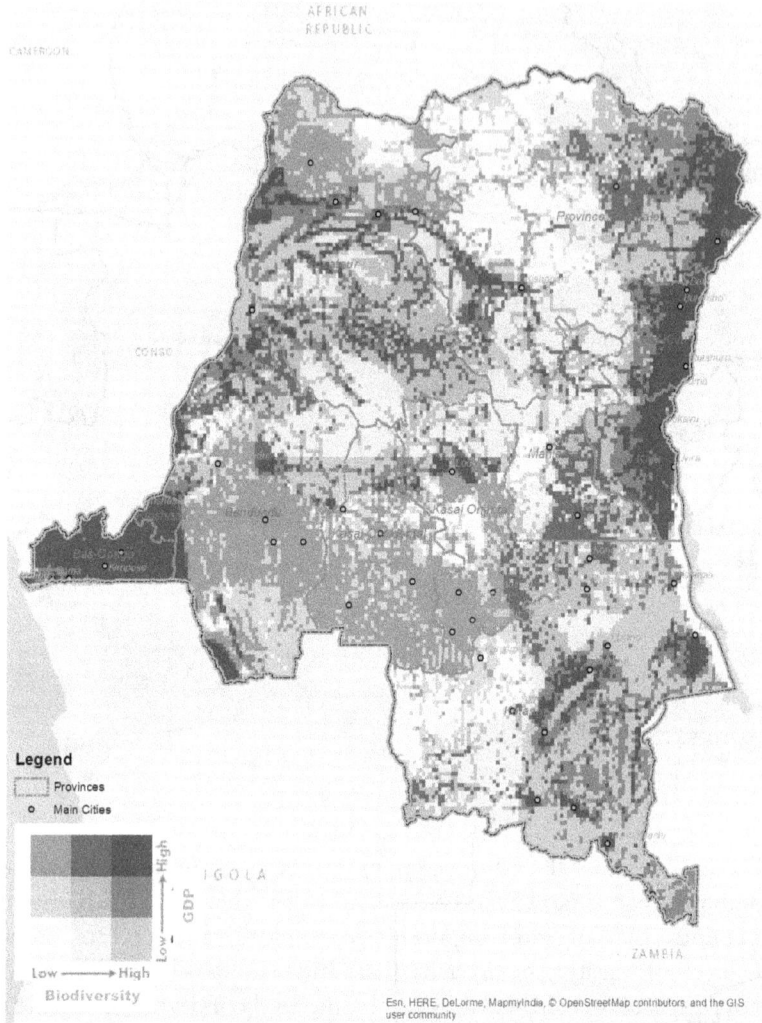

high-quality roads. The aggregate increase in local GDP is estimated to be approximately US$18.1 million per year, a lower bound estimate.[2] In a similar manner, simulations estimate the total deforestation caused by road improvement projects in major urban centers. The estimated additional deforestation due to this project predicts that much of the additional deforestation will occur near the major cities of Kananga, Kisangani, and Maniema, as well as much of the provinces of South Kivu and Maniema. A comparison of GDP and forest loss is presented in map ES.7. For further policy guidance, it is useful to combine these maps to identify high-potential areas, high-risk areas, and areas where there will be complex trade-offs (see map ES.8).

To get a clearer picture of the economic and ecological impact of the major urban center road network improvement project, as a first step, changes in local GDP and deforestation are overlaid to identify areas that would reap the most benefits or face the highest risks of loss.

- Areas in green are "pure benefit" regions, where local GDP gains are very significant and deforestation increases are very low.
- Red areas are the riskiest regions, estimated to have very low local GDP gains but significant deforestation as a result of the project. Protecting these regions would yield the greatest benefits, given that little economic activity would be lost, and there is a significant risk of deforestation.
- The intermediate zone is in yellow.

Map ES.7 Estimated Changes to Local GDP and Deforestation from the Major Urban Center Road Network Improvement Project

a. Estimated local GDP increases

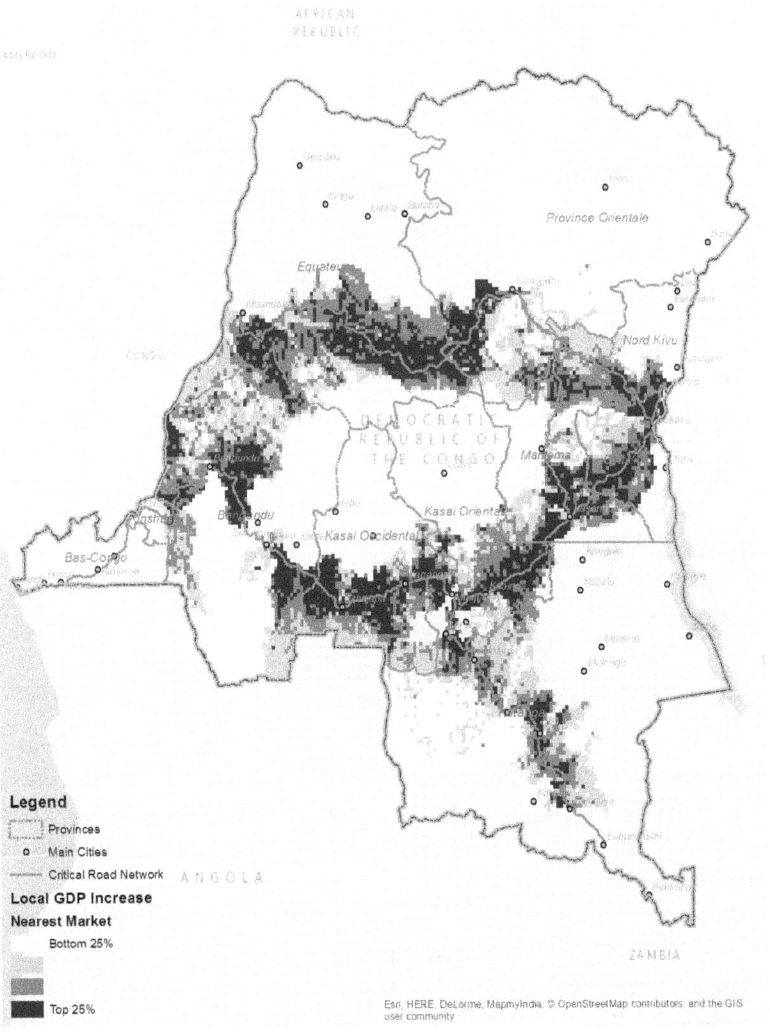

Province Orientale
Nord Kivu
Kasai Oriental
Bas-Congo
ANGOLA
ZAMBIA
Legend
Provinces
Main Cities
Critical Road Network
Local GDP Increase
Nearest Market
Bottom 25%
Top 25%
Esri, HERE, DeLorme, MapmyIndia, © OpenStreetMap contributors, and the GIS user community

map continues next page

Map ES.7 Estimated Changes to Local GDP and Deforestation from the Major Urban Center Road Network Improvement Project *(continued)*

b. Estimated additional deforestation

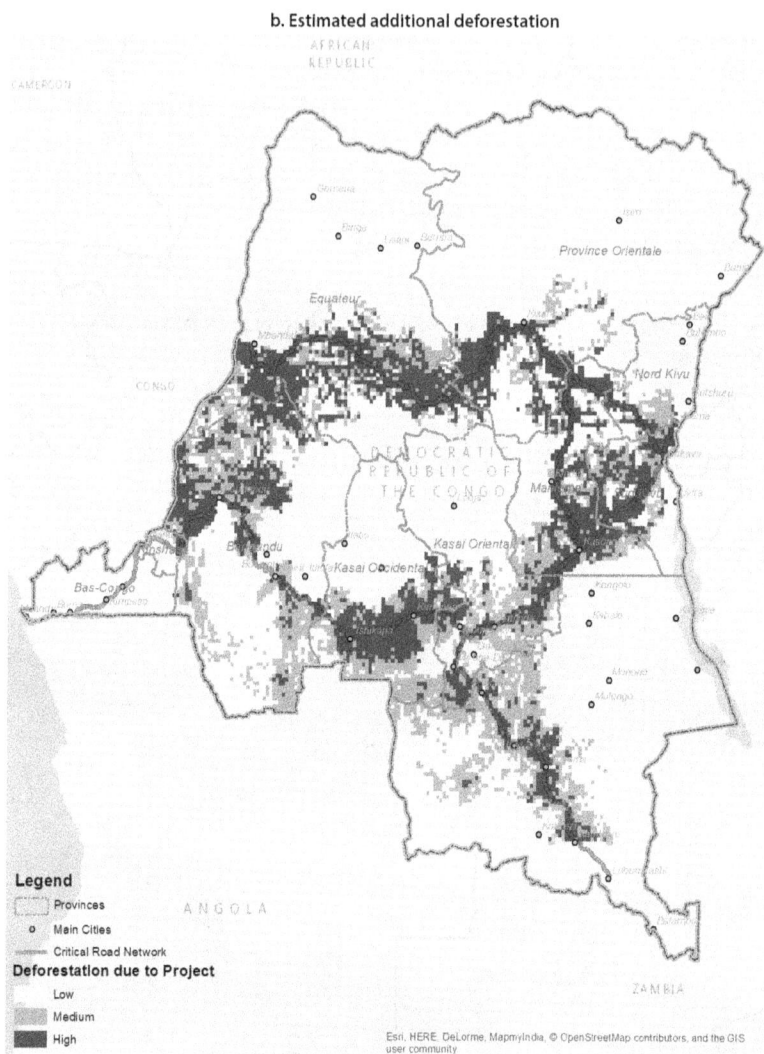

Legend

- Provinces
- Main Cities
- Critical Road Network

Deforestation due to Project

- Low
- Medium
- High

Esri, HERE, DeLorme, MapmyIndia, © OpenStreetMap contributors, and the GIS user community

Sources: Ghosh and others 2010; Hansen and others 2013; and authors' calculations.
Note: GDP = gross domestic product.

An interesting policy implication is that estimated areas of high concern are relatively few and well defined; on the other hand, the trade-off zones and low hazard areas seem larger, suggesting scope for considerable win-wins for the economy and the environment.

To illustrate the utility of this approach at finer spatial scales, the report uses the same techniques to examine the costs and benefits of a much smaller road improvement project, situated around Virunga National Park (maps ES.9 and ES.10). This project would improve a 525 kilometer road that connects the city of Goma, situated just south of Virunga National Park

Map ES.8 Major Urban Center Road Network Deforestation Risk Assessment

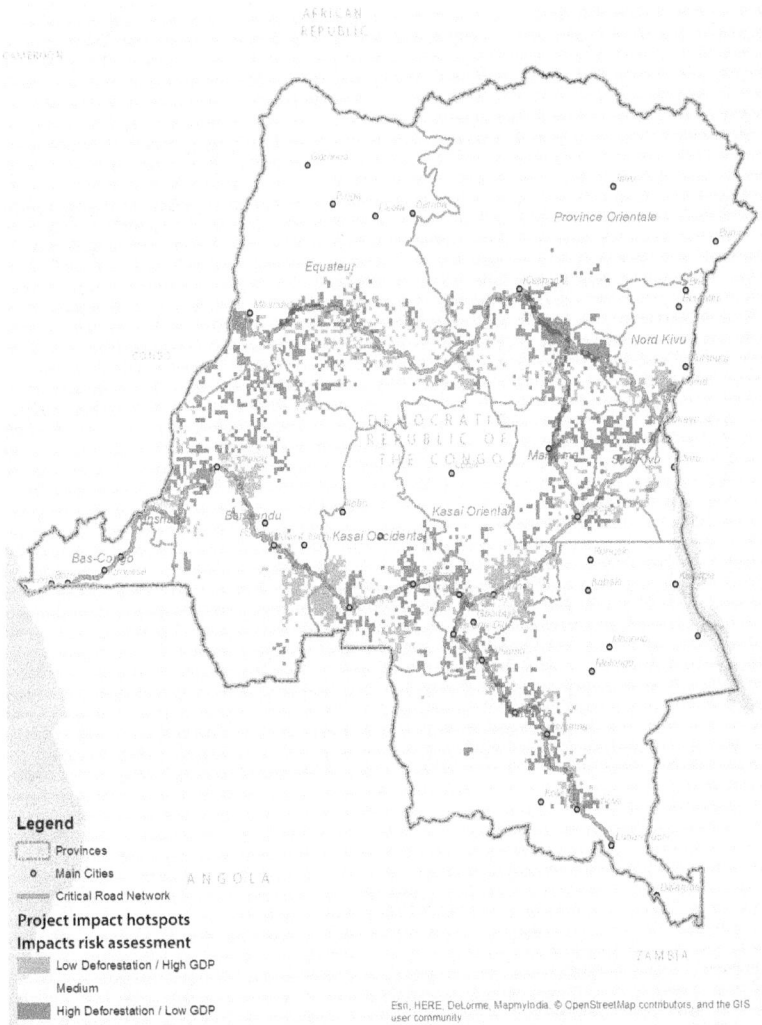

Legend
- Provinces
- Main Cities
- Critical Road Network
- Project impact hotspots

Impacts risk assessment
- Low Deforestation / High GDP
- Medium
- High Deforestation / Low GDP

Source: Hansen and others 2013.

between the park and Lake Kivu, to Bunia, approximately 100 kilometers north of the park, near Lake Albert. Despite being a very populated area (approximately 4.5 million Congolese live within a narrow corridor around the road), the current condition of the road is quite poor, and in many areas it is impassable.

The surrounding area has significant deposits of mineral wealth, including gold and the rare-earth mineral coltan. The land also contains very fertile soils, with theoretical maximum yields that are orders of magnitude greater than current agricultural yields. This road thus appears to be a major candidate for significant investment to spur economic activity. Nevertheless, road infrastructure development in this region may come with deep trade-offs. The land around the potential road project is heavily forested and includes one of the world's most important national parks. Virunga National Park was established in 1924 and was the first designated national park in Africa. Environmental factors aside, Virunga National Park has the potential to become one of the greatest tourist attractions on the continent if the conflict and security issues in the eastern part of the country could be resolved. Destroying this natural capital would be much more than an environmental calamity—it would extinguish a significant source of future income for the country's impoverished inhabitants.

Given the immense trade-offs in this project, it would benefit greatly from the analysis developed in this report. The benefits—the increase in local GDP—are calculated at the pixel level (that is, at the 10 ×10 kilometer level), and aggregated to arrive at a final range of US$7.29 million to US$31.9 million per year above the baseline, depending on whether one uses a local elasticity or the national elasticity calculated in box 2.2 of chapter 2. Map ES.9 shows the distribution of these benefits. Note that they are clustered around the road because the local GDP increase is the intersection of the baseline local GDP and the percentage change in transport costs, both of which are highly clustered around the road. Multiplying these two further magnifies this clustering.

Using the methodology described in this report, the predicted additional deforestation due to the Virunga National Park road improvement project is estimated to see which regions are most at risk. Map ES.10 shows the estimated annual deforestation that would occur due to the road improvement project. The biggest risk to deforestation occurs in those regions that have already shown a propensity to be deforested and that are nearest to the population centers and the improved road. This simulation shows that the areas that would be most stressed are those near Lake Edward, the corridor between Goma and Rutshuru, and the corridor from Katwa to Butembo to Beni. To a much lesser extent, additional deforestation may also occur to the west and northwest of Bunia and to the northwest of Goma.

As a final point, the estimated additional deforestation due to the project is layered on top of the current biodiversity index to see which threatened areas have the most biodiversity and are therefore most worth protecting. This composite is shown in map ES.11. The grid cells outlined in black are those in which deforestation is predicted to increase because of the project. Although this map does not distinguish areas by the intensity of deforestation, it allows the gradient of biodiversity within the affected area to be compared to show which areas are ecologically most important. It is clear that some of the regions with the highest ecological value also coincide with the regions predicted to experience the highest rate of deforestation from the project.

The important conclusion is that the Virunga National Park road project poses an immense risk to the forests and the high-value biodiversity in the region.

Map ES.9 Estimated Changes to Local GDP Due to the Virunga National Park Road Improvement Project

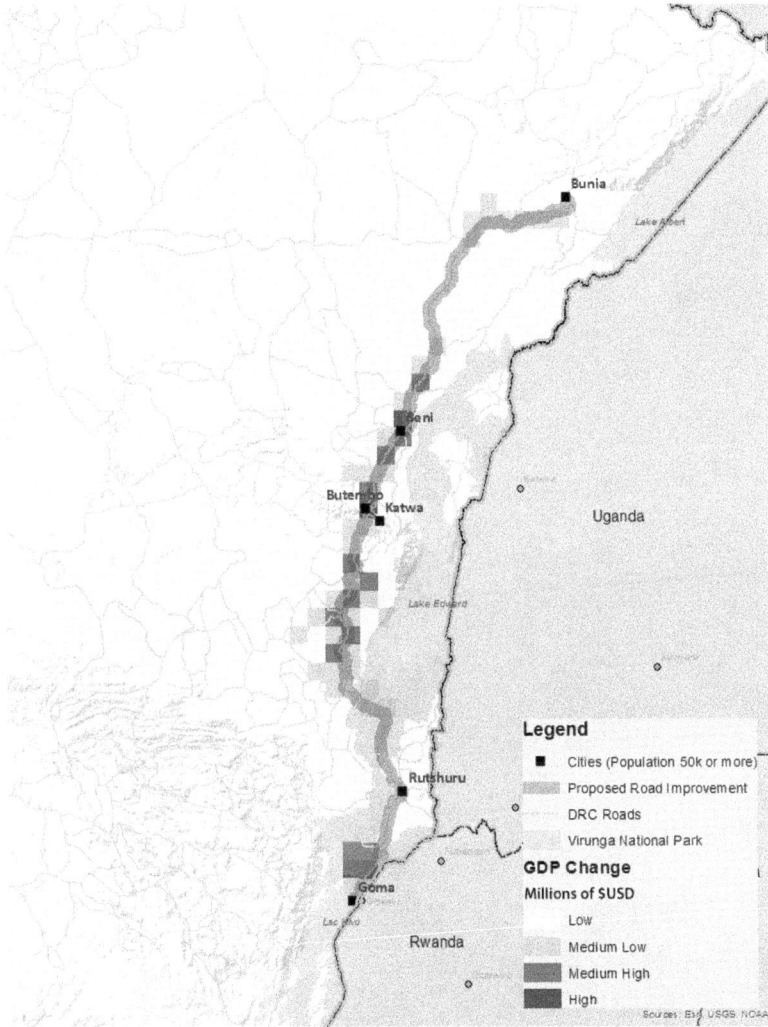

Sources: Ghosh and others 2010; and authors' calculations.
Note: GDP = gross domestic product; DRC = Democratic Republic of Congo.

Before undertaking such a project, stakeholders should carefully compare the estimated benefits with these costs to ensure that the trade-offs are worthwhile and to determine whether and what mitigation strategies are needed. Indeed, as this report highlights, small deviations in the pathway of this road could make an immense difference in generating more economic benefits while safeguarding vulnerable areas. The tools developed here allow for such assessments to be made before a major investment in project appraisal and design occurs.

Map ES.10 Estimated Additional Annual Deforestation Due to the Virunga National Park Road Improvement Project

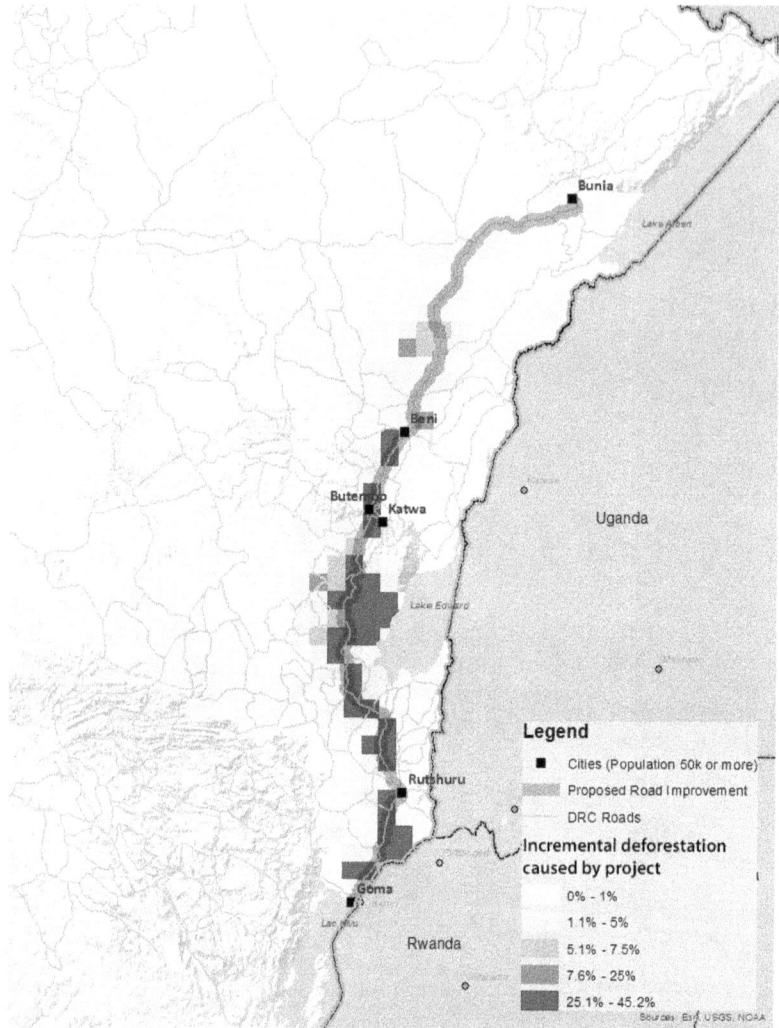

Sources: Hansen and others 2013; and authors' calculations.
Note: DRC = Democratic Republic of Congo.

Map ES.11 Biodiversity Composite Index Compared with Estimated Additional Deforestation Due to the Project

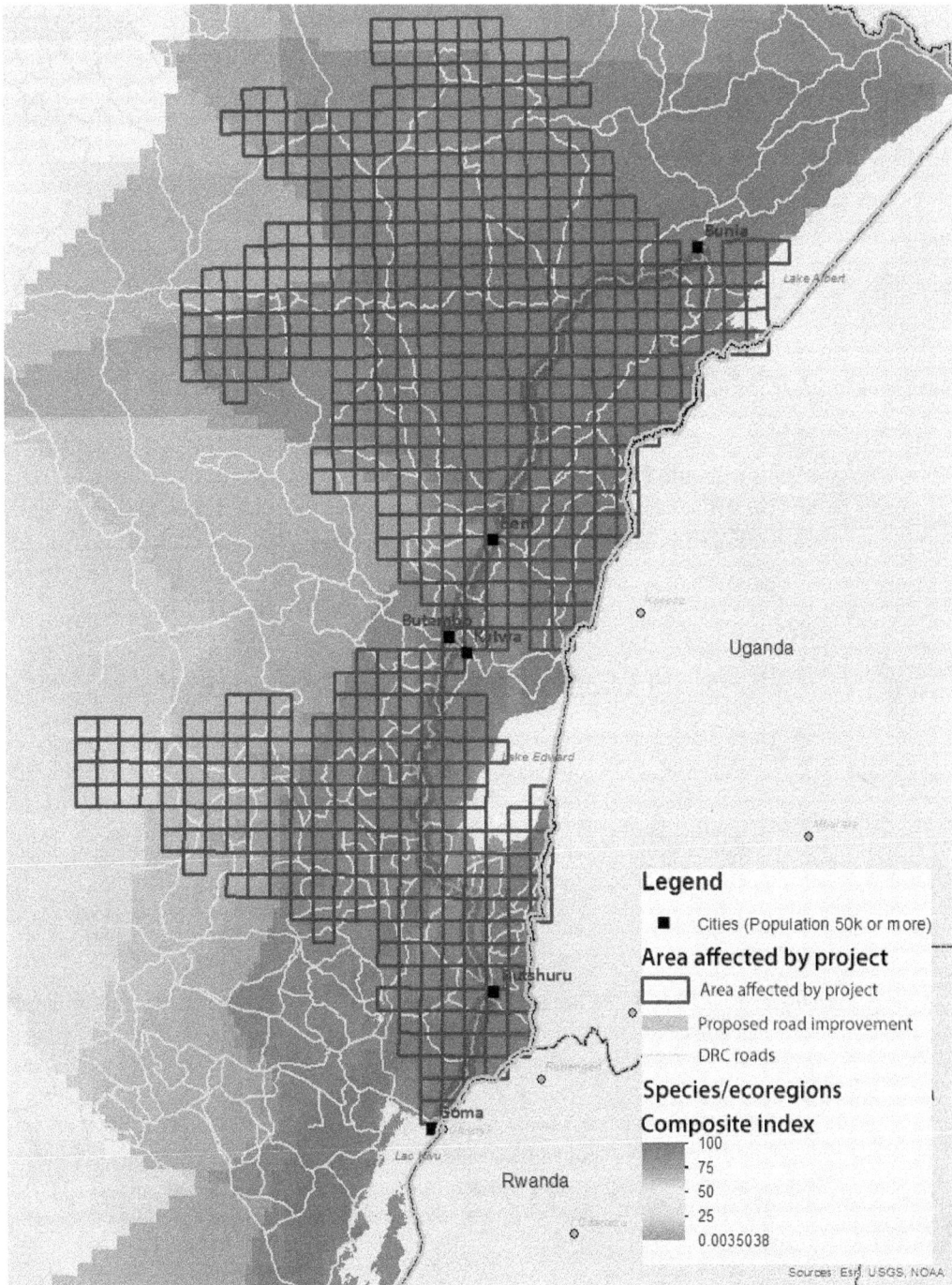

Note: DRC = Democratic Republic of Congo.

Conclusion

Overall, the results suggest that the siting of infrastructure needs to take impacts into consideration at the very outset of the planning process. This report presents both new data and new techniques that can be used to identify areas of opportunity, risk, and potential for REDD+ financing.

Such upstream planning has been rendered both feasible and cost-effective with the availability of georeferenced information on forest cover and economic data. This report provides the data and easily comprehensible maps for such an exercise. The maps provide a simple visual tool that summarizes a computationally intensive exercise. The report demonstrates a procedure for prioritizing investments and identifying hazards, win-wins, and areas where difficult trade-offs may need to occur. The data made available as a result of this exercise could provide valuable information for policies such as REDD+ prioritization and the location of growth poles, agricultural zones, and so on. The approach is perhaps a timely contribution for the Democratic Republic of Congo since much investment is likely to occur in the next few decades. Finally, an important caveat is in order. The results presented here are contingent upon the available data, which is imperfect and limited, so caution needs to be exercised, and the results need to be combined with adequate on-site verification to confirm the accuracy of the results.

Notes

1. The approach uses cross-sectional data on local GDP, transport costs, and several control variables to predict how changes in transport costs affect local GDP.

2. This estimate is made using a partial equilibrium framework, and these benefits are only a subset of the total benefits to reducing transport costs (other benefits include those stemming from improved transport between cities, increased access to multiple cities rather than solely the cheapest one, and better access to ports); therefore, this estimate is likely a very conservative, minimum benefit.

References

Ali, R., A. F. Barra, C. N. Berg, R. Damania, J. D. Nash, and J. Russ. 2015. "Infrastructure in Conflict-Prone and Fragile Environments: Evidence from the Democratic Republic of Congo." Policy Research Working Paper 7273, World Bank, Washington, DC.

De Merode, E., K. Homewood, and G. Cowlishaw. 2003. "Wild Resources and Livelihoods of Poor Households in Democratic Republic of Congo." ODI Wildlife Policy Briefing 1.1, Overseas Development Institute, London.

Ghosh, T., R. L. Powell, C. D. Elvidge, K. E. Baugh, P. C. Sutton, and S. Anderson. 2010. "Shedding Light on the Global Distribution of Economic Activity." *Open Geography Journal* 3 (1): 148–61.

Hansen, M. C., P. V. Potapov, R. Moore, M. Hancher, S. A. Turubanova, A. Tyukavina, D. Thau, S. V. Stehman, S. J. Goetz, T. R. Loveland, A. Kommareddy, A. Egorov, L. Chini, C. O. Justice, and J. R. G. Townshend. 2013. "High-Resolution Global Maps of 21st-Century Forest Cover Change." *Science* 342 (6160): 850–53.

Abbreviations

2SLS	two-stage least squares
EIA	environmental impact assessment
GDP	gross domestic product
GIS	geographic information system
GLS	generalized least squares
IUCN	International Union for Conservation of Nature
IV	instrumental variables
OLS	ordinary least squares
REDD	Reducing Emissions from Deforestation and Forest Degradation
REDD+	Reducing Emissions from Deforestation and Forest Degradation, and fostering conservation, sustainable management of forests, and enhancement of forest carbon stocks
SPAM	Spatial Production Allocation Model
WWF	World Wildlife Fund

CHAPTER 1

Overview

Context and Rationale

The purpose of this study is to demonstrate several techniques that can be used to evaluate pathways to sustainable growth in the Democratic Republic of Congo via infrastructure improvement. Decades of conflict and neglect have left the country's transport infrastructure among the sparsest and most dilapidated in the world. Even by the standards of other low-income countries, road infrastructure is deficient (see table 1.1). In many parts of the country, traveling to the capital, Kinshasa, by road is impossible, making air travel the only way to move around the country. And despite having one of the largest river networks in the world, river transport is often hampered by high levels of silting and long wait times at ports caused by poor infrastructure (Ulimwengu and others 2009). This transport infrastructure deficit reinforces national, provincial, and within-city isolation, causing not just economic problems, but also making it difficult to forge economic and social cohesion.

Although improving infrastructure is by no means a panacea, the Democratic Republic of Congo's infrastructure deficit is a significant constraint to growth. However, determining the optimal location of infrastructure investment in the country is complex, given its geography and socioeconomic structure. First, the vast distances and extreme variations in the spatial distribution of gross domestic product (GDP) (map 1.1) lead to an urgent need for improving interprovincial as well as intraprovincial connectivity to promote trade and economic cohesion. Connecting regions that flourish with those that lag could provide a significant boost to economic growth. Second, the challenge of connectivity is partially alleviated by the Democratic Republic of Congo's vast river network. The waterways are frequently used as a means of transport, connecting areas that are otherwise unconnected by roads. However, this potentially useful mode of transport remains more expensive than it should be (World Bank 2014). Third, the Democratic Republic of Congo has an exceptional endowment of forests that are potentially put at risk from infrastructure improvement and expansion. Given the very high global and local value of the forests, minimizing the potential for their destruction must be a top priority.

Table 1.1 Road Transport in the Democratic Republic of Congo

Indicator	Units	Low-income country average	Congo, Dem. Rep.
Paved road density	km/1,000 km² of land	16	1
Unpaved road density	km/1,000 km² of land	68	14
Paved road traffic	Average annual daily traffic	1,028	257
Unpaved road traffic	Average annual daily traffic	55	20
Perceived transport quality	Share of firms identifying road transport as a major business constraint (percent)	23	30

Source: Foster and Benitez 2011.
Note: km = kilometer.

Map 1.1 Local GDP in the Democratic Republic of Congo, 2006

a. Local GDP in the Democratic Republic of Congo, 2006

Legend

☐ Provinces
○ Main cities

Local GDP
Million US$ per 10km²
<0.5
0.6–1.0
1.1–5.0
5.1–10.0
10.1–100.0
>100

Esri, HERE, DeLorme, MapmyIndia, © OpenStreetMap contributors, and the GIS user community

map continues next page

Map 1.1 Local GDP in the Democratic Republic of Congo, 2006 *(continued)*

b. Regional disparities shown by three-dimensional map of
local GDP in the Democratic Republic of Congo

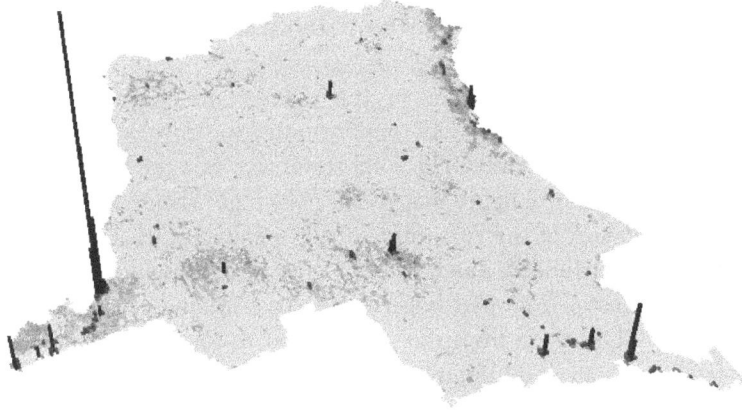

Source: Ghosh and others 2010.
Note: GDP = gross domestic product.

Finally, frequent conflict, which pervades the eastern portion of the country, can potentially limit or negate entirely any infrastructure investments made there, and must be taken into account.

Natural Resources, Infrastructure, and Development

Despite being one of the poorest countries in the region, the Democratic Republic of Congo contains vast economic potential within its borders. The country's natural resource endowment in the form of land, minerals, and forests is unparalleled. The agricultural sector, which is by far the most important sector for employment, generates about 40 percent of total income and employs 60 percent of the workforce. Nevertheless, agricultural productivity (output per worker) has declined dramatically since independence in 1960 (Fulginiti and others 2004). This decline has led to a steep reduction in agricultural exports and in food availability, leading to more than 70 percent of the population being food insecure, and nearly one-fourth of the population being chronically malnourished (Ulimwengu and others 2009).

Despite this historic decline, sustainable expansion of the agricultural industry remains achievable. Currently, only 10 percent of arable land is farmed, and only 13,000 hectares are irrigated as compared with the potential for 4 million hectares. With more than 22.5 million hectares of low-population-density, uncultivated, unprotected, nonforested land, there is considerable room for expansion with little pressure on forests (Deininger and Byerlee 2011). With proper management and stewardship of the land, the Democratic Republic of Congo could become the breadbasket of Africa and feed upward of a billion people. Strong evidence indicates that reducing travel times to markets could have a significant effect on agricultural production. Dorosh and others (2010) show a strong, plausibly causal effect between these variables using data from all of Sub-Saharan Africa. Ulimwengu and others (2009), in a similar study, focus solely on the Democratic Republic of Congo and find that reducing travel time to the nearest city of 50,000 residents by 10.0 percent increases crop production by 4.4 percent.

Mining, another pivotal sector in the Democratic Republic of Congo's economy, also presents tremendous opportunities for development. Currently accounting for 12 percent of GDP, some estimates put the country's mineral wealth at US$24 trillion, a figure that is especially high when compared with the average income levels of the two-thirds of the population that subsists on less than US$1 per day.[1] Indeed, much of the Democratic Republic of Congo's current income is clustered around large mining sites. Map 1.1 shows the spatial distribution of GDP. Aside from the area around Kinshasa, significant peaks in income can be seen around Lubumbashi, the country's mining capital, with enormous deposits of copper and cobalt; Mbuji-Mayi, an area rich in diamonds; and Kivu, which has large deposits of gold and other rare-earth metals. The Democratic Republic of Congo's economic success is heavily influenced by this sector.

The familiar resource-curse challenges, coupled with low investment and lack of infrastructure, have prevented the Democratic Republic of Congo from taking full advantage of its mineral wealth. Although tapping mineral reserves offers the prospect of poverty alleviation and growth, it also comes with risks. Much of the country's mineral deposits are located in the eastern part of the country. These mines are geographically isolated and are located in areas that are subject to frequent conflict from local militias. Indeed, the very presence of the mineral deposits both causes these conflicts and generates the economic windfall necessary to perpetuate them. Improving transport infrastructure near these mines, although necessary to spur economic growth, could possibly further fuel these conflicts, both by facilitating the movement of resources out of the region and by reducing rebel groups' travel costs (Ali and others 2015). When analyzing the impacts of future road construction, this study accounts for this possibility by factoring in the effects of recent conflicts.

Finally, perhaps the Democratic Republic of Congo's most valuable natural resource is its forests. Home to more than 145 million hectares of rain forests, the country has the second-largest forest endowment in the world, and contains more than 60 percent of the total forest area in the Congo Basin. These forests are of great global importance because they constitute the second-largest carbon sink in the world and have tremendous biodiversity value. The forests are also of paramount importance to local welfare. Up to 40 percent of individuals living in forested provinces rely on hunting, gathering, and fishing as their main sources of food (De Merode, Homewood, and Cowlishaw 2003). Recent data from the Center for International Forestry Research's Poverty Environment Network show that environmental dependence (that is, the share of income that households derive from environmental sources) is as high as 45 percent for the country's poorest families and tends to decline as incomes increase (see figure 1.1).

Figure 1.1 Environmental Income Dependence by Income Quintile

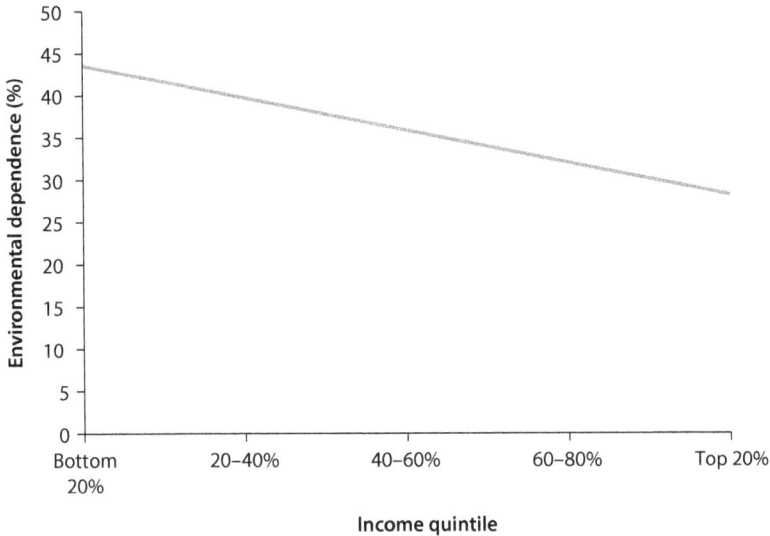

Source: Data from CIFOR's Poverty Environment Network (PEN) survey. See Angelsen and others 2014 for more details on this survey.
Note: Environmental dependence is the ratio of environment-derived income to total household income. Ratio is calculated for each income quintile, and the best-fit line is shown.

This finding implies that the incomes of the most vulnerable households in the country could be jeopardized if the forests are not properly managed and protected.

Although the deforestation rate in the Democratic Republic of Congo is currently the highest in the Congo Basin, at about 0.22 percent annually between 2000 and 2005 (Megevand 2013), it is still low compared with South America and Southeast Asia, whose net deforestation rates are, respectively, two and four times higher. The country's relatively low deforestation rates cannot be entirely attributed to successful public policy, however. Deforestation and degradation have been limited by a combination of factors—conflict, political instability, and poor infrastructure—that have created a kind of "passive protection" of the forest. A vast literature has shown that deforestation tends to occur near roads.[2] Therefore, the location of new road construction or improvement in the country must be chosen carefully so that, for a unit cost, it maximizes net welfare benefits. This calculation must include both greater economic benefits from reduced transport costs and increased connectivity, and minimized costs from deforestation and biodiversity loss.

Structure of the Report

This report attempts to take a holistic approach to evaluating the impact of road network improvement. Chapter 2 provides an overview of the current state of the Democratic Republic of Congo's transport system. Using a geospatial model, the critical portions of the system are identified, and the economic benefits from reducing local transport costs are estimated. Chapter 3 examines the potential deforestation that could occur from infrastructure investments. Estimates of total forest loss are explored, as well as possible biodiversity impacts that this loss may have on the local biome. Finally, chapter 4 combines these two analyses by simulating the effects of two road improvement projects: one connecting major urban centers to Kinshasa and another dealing with a specific road improvement project in the east of the country. Economic benefits due to local transport cost reductions are estimated, as are costs in the form of additional forest depletion. The results of this simulation are meant to give policy makers one additional tool to help them prioritize infrastructure investment projects.

In sum, this report presents both new information and new tools that can be used by policy makers for broad planning purposes to determine where investments yield the highest net returns and how damage to valuable natural assets could be avoided. Thus, this work considerably advances the information that is available to planners, suggests sophisticated methodologies that could be used to guide decisions, and provides a more informed foundation upon which to deliberate and decide upon issues that inevitably involve trade-offs when financial resources are limited.

Notes

1. "UNEP Study Confirms DR Congo's Potential as Environmental Powerhouse but Warns of Critical Threats" (http://www.unep.org/newscentre/Default.aspx ?DocumentID=2656&ArticleID=8890).
2. Several notable papers include Cropper, Puri, and Griffiths (2001) in Thailand; Chomitz and Gray (1996) in Belize; and Gaveau and others (2009) in Indonesia.

References

Ali, R., A. F. Barra, C. N. Berg, R. Damania, J. D. Nash, and J. Russ. 2015. "Infrastructure in Conflict-Prone and Fragile Environments: Evidence from the Democratic Republic of Congo." Policy Research Working Paper 7273, World Bank, Washington, DC.

Angelsen, A., Pamela Jagger, Ronnie Babigumira, Brian Belcher, Nicholas J. Hogarth, Simone Bauch, Jan Börner, Carsten Smith-Hall, and Sven Wunder. 2014. "Environmental Income and Rural Livelihoods: A Global-Comparative Analysis." World Development 64 (1): S12–28. http://dx.doi.org/10.1016/j.worlddev.2014 .03.006.

Chomitz, Kenneth M., and David A. Gray. 1996. "Roads, Land Use, and Deforestation: A Spatial Model Applied to Belize." World Bank Economic Review 10(3): 487–512.

Cropper, Maureen, Jyotsna Puri, and Charles Griffiths. 2001. "Predicting the Location of Deforestation: The Role of Roads and Protected Areas in North Thailand." Land Economics 77(2): 172–86.

Deininger, Klaus W., and Derek Byerlee. 2011. Rising Global Interest in Farmland: Can It Yield Sustainable and Equitable Benefits? Washington, DC: World Bank.

De Merode, E., K. Homewood, and G. Cowlishaw. 2003. "Wild Resources and Livelihoods of Poor Households in Democratic Republic of Congo." ODI Wildlife Policy Briefing 1.1, Overseas Development Institute, London.

Dorosh, Paul, Hyoung-Gun Wang, Liang You, and Emily Schmidt. 2010. "Crop Production and Road Connectivity in Sub-Saharan Africa: A Spatial Analysis." World Bank Policy Research Working Paper, World Bank, Washington, DC.

Foster, Vivien, and Daniel Benitez. 2011. "The Democratic Republic of Congo's Infrastructure: A Continental Perspective." World Bank Policy Research Working Paper 5602, World Bank, Washington, DC.

Fulginiti, Lilyan E., Richard K. Perrin, and Bingxin Yu. 2004. "Institutions and Agricultural Productivity in Sub-Saharan Africa." *Agricultural Economics* 31 (2–3): 169–180.

Gaveau, David L. A., Serge Wich, Justin Epting, Daniel Juhn, Markku Kanninen, and Nigel Leader-Williams. 2009. "The Future of Forests and Orangutans (*Pongo abelii*) in Sumatra: Predicting Impacts of Oil Palm Plantations, Road Construction, and Mechanisms for Reducing Carbon Emissions from Deforestation." *Environmental Research Letters* 4 (3): 034013.

Ghosh, T., R. L. Powell, C. D. Elvidge, K. E. Baugh, P. C. Sutton, and S. Anderson. 2010. "Shedding Light on the Global Distribution of Economic Activity." *Open Geography Journal* 3 (1): 148–61.

Megevand, Carole. 2013. *Deforestation Trends in the Congo Basin: Reconciling Economic Growth and Forest Protection*. World Bank: Washington, DC.

Ulimwengu, John, Jose Funes, Derek D. Headey, and Lianghzhi You. 2009. "Paving the Way for Development. The Impact of Transport Infrastructure on Agricultural Production and Poverty Reduction in the Democratic Republic of Congo." International Food Policy Research Institute Discussion Paper 840, International Food Policy Research Institute, Washington, DC.

World Bank. 2014. *Democratic Republic of the Congo River and Urban Transport Review*. Report ACS9800. Washington, DC: World Bank.

CHAPTER 2

A Snapshot of the Democratic Republic of Congo's Transport System

Introduction

The Congolese transport system is a multimodal system with the Congo River as its spine. Much of the Democratic Republic of Congo relies on a combination of roads and rivers to transport people and goods. In some parts of the country, including much of Equateur province, roads have either never existed or have deteriorated so much that river transport is the only means of travel. Several railway lines connect Kinshasa with Kasai and Katanga provinces. However, the service on these lines is often unpredictable and slow, making shipment of perishable goods a dubious and uncertain endeavor. Much of the current transport system was established during the country's colonial period and was developed for the purpose of rapidly exporting raw materials (mainly rubber, ivory, minerals, and timber) from the country's interior. The system gave little regard to the socioeconomic integration of the Congolese territory.

With more than 25,000 kilometers of waterways, the Democratic Republic of Congo has one of the largest networks of navigable routes in the world. Better use of river and lake transport could be one of the keys to economic development and poverty alleviation, chiefly because it is cheap and serves most of the interior portion of the country, which has high agricultural potential. It also complements, or in some cases substitutes for, road transport in the other major regions of the country. Kisangani, the third-largest city, and Mbandaka, the capital of the important province of Equateur, are connected to the capital, Kinshasa, only by river transport.

The exploitation of river and lake transport, which until 1971 was virtually a public enterprise monopoly, is now dominated by numerous formal and informal private operators. The largest port in the country is in Kinshasa and handles about 2 million tons of cargo per year. For comparison, this single port carries more than triple the volume transported by the national railway, SNCC. River transport is essential for the development of agriculture, which has become the center of the government's economic development strategy, because it would allow the country's immense rural areas to be opened up.

In this chapter, several analyses are performed to identify the most crucial parts of the country's transport network by analyzing the effectiveness of roads and rivers as transport modes to the nearest markets and to Kinshasa. The analysis generally finds that although roads are important for local transport to a nearby city, the overall road network is far too incomplete for longer distance transport to be viable. For transport over long distances, the river system is vital. Even with the current poor state of port infrastructure, traffic is still able to traverse the rivers for much of the year. Thus, the river has become a last resort in many areas in which the more infrastructure-intensive road and railway transport networks have broken down or never existed. Finally, the chapter demonstrates a methodology for estimating some of the economic benefits of road construction.

The Current State of the Transport Network

An Overview

This chapter discusses a geospatial model that has been developed to identify costs of and bottlenecks to travel. The model simulates how individuals and traded goods are moved around the Democratic Republic of Congo. Taking the road and river network (including information on both location and quality), land topography, and population data as inputs, the model makes several plausible assumptions about how local farmers, traders, and other economic agents will move around the country. The model culminates in an algorithm that estimates the transport routes that a cost minimizer would take to ship products to market, to and from any location within the country. The assessment ultimately identifies the existing portions of the road network that are both most crucial to the current network and also most in need of rehabilitation. Box 2.1 provides more information on the geospatial model.

As stated, this model includes two modes of transport: roads and rivers. The third type of ground transport used in the Democratic Republic of Congo, railways, is excluded because it serves very local areas and provides sporadic service, which limits its economic reliability.

Local Transport to the Nearest Market

Improving access to local markets would be beneficial for several reasons: increased opportunities and lower costs for farmers to sell their crops, increased access to productive inputs, and increased access to local services such as schools and hospitals, among many others. Given the importance of local trade to rural farmers, it is natural to begin with an analysis of local transport to the nearest market.

Two images are shown in map 2.1. Panel a shows the costs of transporting goods to the cheapest market from every location within the Democratic

---

Box 2.1 Geospatial Model

The analysis in this chapter is based on the findings of a geospatial model constructed to simulate how products and people move around the Democratic Republic of Congo. A geospatial model was chosen over other means of analysis, such as household surveys, because it allows for analysis in every part of the country, not just where the surveyed households are located. It also allows for a richer analysis given the limited household survey data available for the country.

The construction of this model involves two steps. First, data describing the transport network were assembled. This process involved collecting data about the road and river network and the location of ports. Next, assumptions were made about how people and products will move around this network. These two steps are discussed below, followed by a section describing the caveats of using this model.

Transport Network

The foundation of the geospatial model is that it allows the travel costs between any two points within the Democratic Republic of Congo to be calculated. Once that cost is determined, transport routes can be calculated under the assumption that agents will minimize transport costs. The first step is to take account of the quality and condition of the existing transport infrastructure.

These data were collected from various sources. Road location data were obtained from Delorme, a company that specializes in global positioning system mapping software and that has one of the most thorough road network maps available for the Democratic Republic of Congo. Road quality was obtained from the Africa Infrastructure Country Diagnostic, which provides information such as the width of each road, whether it is paved or unpaved, and its condition. Data on which rivers are navigable were obtained from the UN Food and Agriculture Organization and the Democratic Republic of Congo's Ministère des Infrastructures, Travaux Publics et Reconstruction, and the locations of river ports were obtained from the UN's Joint Logistics Centre.

Model Assumptions

Once the transport network was constructed, informed assumptions were made about the cost of moving around the network. The Highway Development and Management Model[a] was used to estimate the cost of the road network. This model, which is commonly used by engineers, takes into account the roughness of the terrain and quality and condition of the road, as well as country-level factors (such as price of fuel, average quality of the fleet, price of a used truck, and wages), to determine the unit cost of traveling along every segment of the road network (for more details, see Ali and others 2015). World Bank (2014) provided the cost of traveling along the river and the cost of loading the products onto a boat.

Once the costs of moving people and products around the country were known, the likely transport routes used by the Congolese could be simulated. The points of origin for the analysis were created by dividing the territory into more than 27,000 cells of

box continues next page

Box 2.1 Geospatial Model *(continued)*

approximately 10 kilometers on a side and estimating their centroid. Then, transport cost to the local market was estimated by calculating every possible transport route from every cell centroid to every possible market, and selecting the cheapest route-market combination as the most likely route to a destination. A market is defined in this report as a city of 50,000 or more residents. This threshold was chosen because it identifies both the major and smaller cities in the country, and it is also consistent with much of the transport literature in Africa. Finally, this model can be used as an input into statistical analysis, as is described in box 2.2.

Model Caveats

Although it is believed that this model simulates how people and products move around the Democratic Republic of Congo as accurately as possible, some shortcomings must be acknowledged. First, the model does not factor in the cost of delays at ports or along the roads or rivers. Transport in the country, especially along the river, can take significantly longer than might be expected because of dilapidated infrastructure (such as roads that are washed away during the rainy season), river silting (which can make segments of some rivers impassable, especially during the dry season), or other human factors (such as low capacity and skills at shipyards, or port operators making suboptimal staffing decisions because they lack information on supply and demand for transport) (World Bank 2014). Without proper estimates of the opportunity cost of time, the model likely underestimates the true cost of using the river, which is relatively cheap in a pecuniary sense, but costs a significant amount of time. Cost estimates for using the roads also include only pecuniary costs; however, time delays along the roads are significantly lower on average than time delays for using the river.

Finally, although the model includes the two most common methods of transport—roads and rivers—other methods for transporting people or products around the Democratic Republic of Congo are available. Several railroad lines do exist; however, they service small portions of the country, mostly in the Kasai and Katanga provinces, and are notoriously unreliable. Air travel is also used quite commonly to travel between provinces. Because of its cost, however, this is not a viable option for most Congolese citizens (World Bank 2014).

a. For a discussion of the model, see http://www.piarc.org/en/knowledge-base/road-assets-management/HDM-4-Software/.

Republic of Congo (a market is defined as a city of at least 50,000 residents), using a multimodal model with access to both roads and rivers.[1] Panel b shows the difference in costs between a unimodal (road-only model) and the multimodal model, and thus shows the areas that are most likely to use and benefit from using the river for transport. It is clear from these maps that, aside from some isolated areas in the northwest part of the country, rivers are used relatively infrequently for local transport. Specifically, only 14 percent of individuals in the country live in areas where it would be cost-effective to use river transport for any portion of their trip to the local

Map 2.1 Transport Cost to Cheapest Market

a. Cost of transporting goods to the nearest market using a multimodal system

b. The difference in transportation costs to the cheapest market between a unimodal and multimodal system

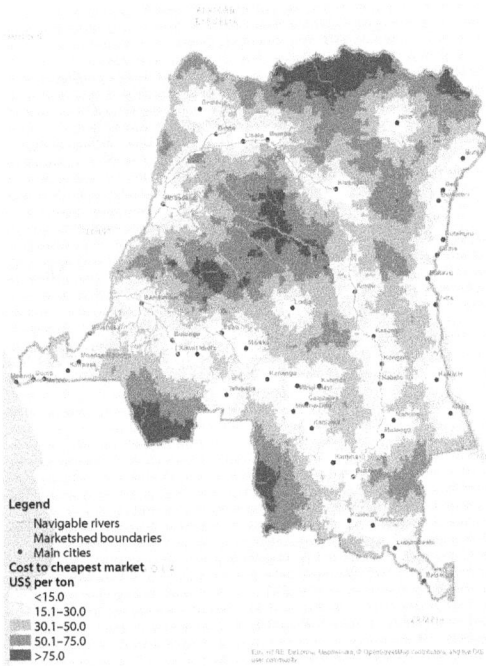

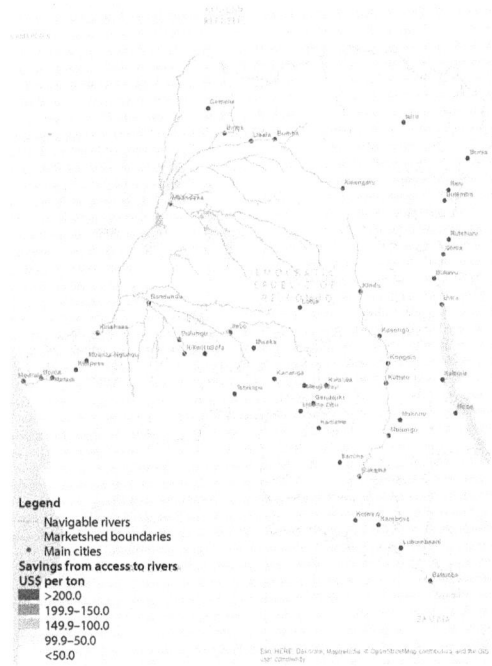

Legend
Navigable rivers
Marketshed boundaries
• Main cities
Cost to cheapest market
US$ per ton
<15.0
15.1–30.0
30.1–50.0
50.1–75.0
>75.0

Legend
Navigable rivers
Marketshed boundaries
• Main cities
Savings from access to rivers
US$ per ton
>200.0
199.9–150.0
149.9–100.0
99.9–50.0
<50.0

Note: Panel a shows the transport cost to the cheapest market for every region within the Democratic Republic of Congo, given a multimodal (road and river) model. Panel b shows the difference in transport costs between this multimodal model, and a unimodal, roads only, model, and thus shows the regions where river transport is most important.

market. Furthermore, these individuals live in areas that account for only about 7 percent of the country's gross domestic product (GDP), suggesting that investments in river transport will not have a significant impact on local market transport, given the current economic geography of the country. Based on these facts, the road network is likely to be much more important for local transport than are the rivers.

Transport to Kinshasa

Transport costs to the national capital, Kinshasa, are summarized in map 2.2. Access to Kinshasa is important for connectivity and social cohesion. Not only is the capital home to more than 10 percent of the country's population, but it is also a center of wealth and economic activity, making it a vital demand center for rural farmers and other traders from much of the country.

Given the long distance between most of the country and Kinshasa, and the fact that the country's road network is fractured, travel along rivers becomes important to the overall transport network for access to Kinshasa. Map 2.2 (panel a) shows the cost of transporting goods to Kinshasa using both roads and

Map 2.2 Transport Cost to Kinshasa

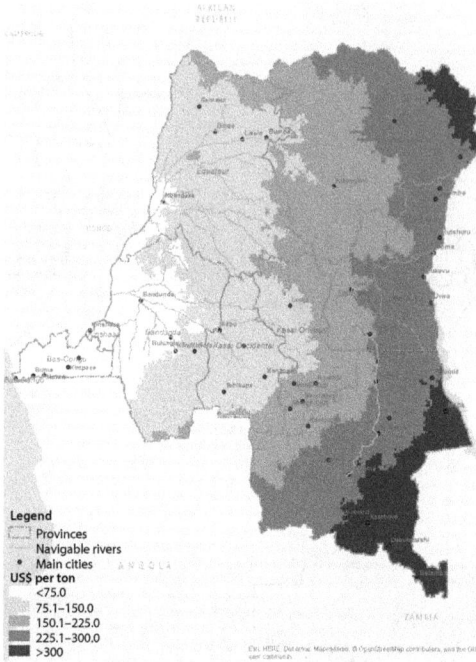

a. Cost of transporting goods to	b. The difference in transportation costs to
Kinshasa using a multimodal system	Kinshasa between a unimodal and multimodal system

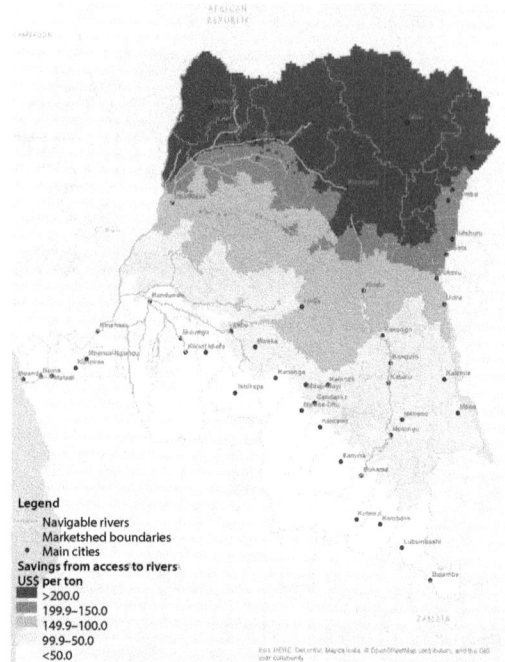

Legend
  Provinces
  Navigable rivers
  • Main cities
US$ per ton
  <75.0
  75.1–150.0
  150.1–225.0
  225.1–300.0
  >300

Legend
  Navigable rivers
  Marketshed boundaries
  • Main cities
Savings from access to rivers
US$ per ton
  >200.0
  199.9–150.0
  149.9–100.0
  99.9–50.0
  <50.0

Note: Panel a shows the transport cost to Kinshasa for every region within the Democratic Republic of Congo, given a multimodal (road and river) model. Panel b shows the difference in transport costs between this multimodal model and a unimodal, roads only, model, and thus shows the regions for which river transport is most important.

rivers in the most efficient manner. As is expected, the cost tends to increase as the origin point moves away from Kinshasa, and also tends to be lower in the northwestern part of the country, which is heavily serviced by tributaries of the Congo River. Panel b of map 2.2 shows the transport cost difference between the multimodal model and the unimodal, roads-only model.

Access to river transport is, as always, more important for longer-distance travel and for goods with a relative low value-to-bulk ratio. Hence, there is a significant difference between the mode of transport that is important for travel to local markets and that used for transport to Kinshasa. When minimizing travel costs, the geospatial model indicates that approximately 80 percent of the population would prefer to use river travel, at least in part, to transport goods to Kinshasa. Moreover, these individuals live in areas that account for nearly 60 percent of the country's GDP. Relative to the 14 percent of individuals and 7 percent of GDP that are in areas that use rivers to transport goods to the local market, it is clear that the river is much more important for long-distance transport to Kinshasa.

Whereas cost savings for transport to local markets are quite low and restricted to areas right along the river, as shown in map 2.1, cost savings for transport to Kinshasa are much greater and accrue throughout much of the country, save the southern part, which is mostly outside the Congo Basin. The northern part of the country is particularly dependent on river transport for reaching Kinshasa, which is not surprising considering that much of this region has no direct road access to Kinshasa.

Two Transport Network Improvement Proposals

The Congo River and its tributaries act as a backbone for shipping goods to Kinshasa. Facilitating access to the river ports that can connect the Congolese to the capital may therefore be a short-term priority for any infrastructure improvement program. For individuals who do not live directly on a navigable and connected river, or live in areas without river ports, the road network becomes an important first leg of the journey for connecting them to a port and, eventually, Kinshasa.

For long-term growth and integration, however, improving access to river ports is insufficient. The volumes of freight transported by river are already significant and continue to grow. However, river transport remains unreliable and much more expensive than it should be. As an example, a trip from Kisangani to Kinshasa over river can take up to two weeks (World Bank 2014). Therefore, in addition to a competitive inland waterway transport system, an efficient, complementary road system is needed to serve segments of the market for which waterway transport is not a viable option (for example, passenger transport or transport of light-weight, high-value goods). Connecting the entire country with a fully integrated road network should therefore be an important priority. To meet these needs, a major urban center road network is proposed, which would connect 11 major urban centers throughout the country with the national capital, Kinshasa.

Improving Access to River Ports

Some segments of the road network leading to ports will be more important than others. Map 2.3 displays roads that connect large population agglomerations,[2] such as Kisangani, Lubumbashi, and the provinces of North and South Kivu, to the river network. Collectively, these roads provide connectivity for up to 60 percent of the population. Focusing on infrastructure that improves these routes, as well as infrastructure at the ports at which they end, will likely have a large positive impact on connectivity relative to other transport projects.

Major Urban Center Road Network

In the coming years, one of the key priorities of the government of the Democratic Republic of Congo is to connect major urban centers with well-maintained, high-quality roads. Map 2.4 identifies the primary roads that would need to be improved or completed to ensure that these urban centers are connected while minimizing the size of the network. This network

Map 2.3 Critical Roads for the Port Network

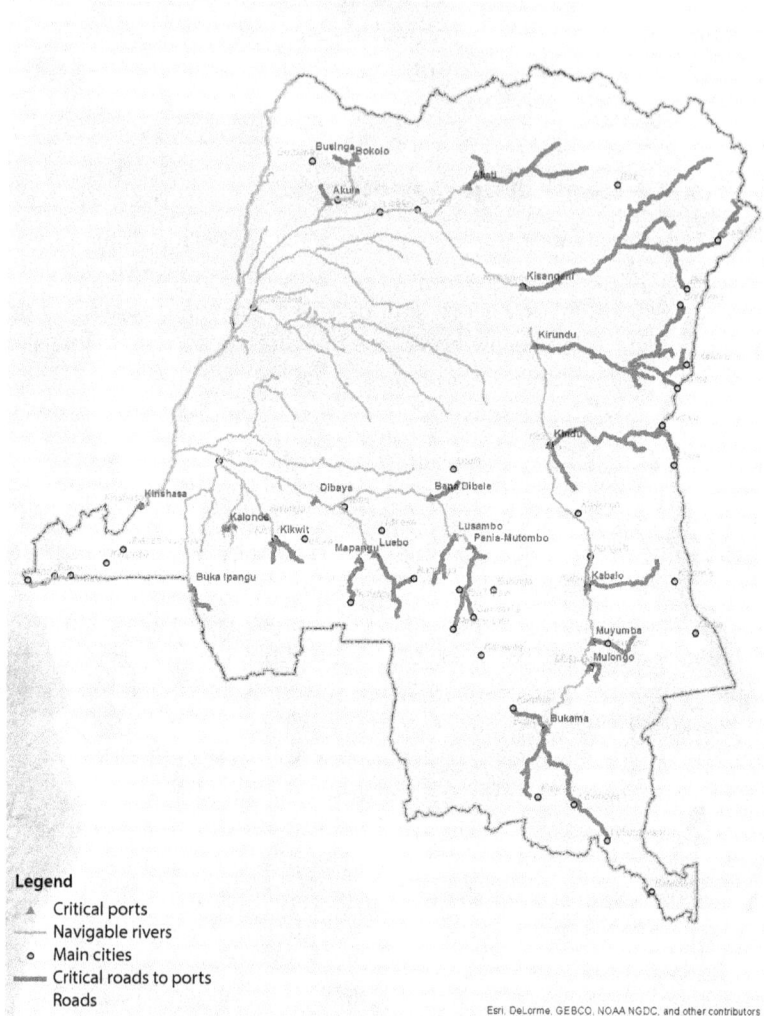

Legend
- ▲ Critical ports
- — Navigable rivers
- ○ Main cities
- ▬ Critical roads to ports
- ▬ Roads

Esri, DeLorme, GEBCO, NOAA NGDC, and other contributors

includes 6,500 kilometers of roads. To put this number in context, the roads in the network would be nearly as long as the entire Sahel, from Dakar, Senegal, to Khartoum, Sudan. Additionally, only 20 percent of the roads in this major urban center road network are currently paved, and 75 percent of all roads are currently in poor condition. Although a tremendous investment in infrastructure would be required to connect these urban centers to Kinshasa, which may not be feasible at the moment, any long-term infrastructure plan should include this as an important priority for improving national cohesion. Chapter 4 presents a simulation of the geolocation of the benefits of this potential project.

Map 2.4 Major Urban Center Road Network

Legend
- ○ Province capital
- ⬚ Provinces
- ▬ Critical road network
- — Navigable rivers
- — Roads

Esri, HERE, DeLorme, Mapmyindia, © OpenStreetMap contributors, and the GIS user community

Benefits to Road Improvement

This section uses regression analysis to determine the economic effects of reducing local transport costs along roads. The approach follows Ali and others (2015) by using cross-sectional data on local GDP, transport costs, and several control variables to predict how changes in transport cost affect local GDP. See box 2.2 for a more thorough explanation of this model.

The results from the regressions show that significant benefits would be derived from decreasing local transport costs, especially in the highest-cost, more densely populated regions. Specifically, a 10 percent reduction in local transport costs would lead to, on average, a 0.46 percent increase in local GDP. Ali and

Box 2.2 The Effect of Transport Costs on Economic Activity

To determine the effect of transport costs on economic activity, this report relies on regression analysis. The analysis very closely follows that of Ali and others (2015). The entire country is divided up into grid cells of approximately 10 kilometers on a side. Each grid cell is a unit of observation in the following model:

$$\ln (Y_i) = \beta_0 + \beta_1 \ln (TM_i) + X_i \gamma + \varepsilon_i, \qquad (2.2.1)$$

in which Y_i denotes local GDP, according to Ghosh and others (2010), in grid cell i. TM_i is the transport cost to market, and X_i is a vector of regional controls. Those controls include ln(population), ln(population)^2, ln(cassava potential yield), ln(cassava potential)^2, ln(distance to nearest mine), and a measure of conflict near the grid cell and the local market. To account for the endogeneity of both market cost and the conflict variables, this report follows Ali and others (2015) and takes an instrumental variable approach. (See Ali and others [2015] for details on the instrumental variables used and a discussion of the conflict measures.)

The results are shown in table B2.2.1. Because all variables are in log form, the estimated coefficients can be interpreted as elasticities. The results in the two-stage least squares model (column 2) show that a 10 percent decline in transport costs to the local market would lead to a 0.46 percent increase in local GDP. Additionally, the regression shows that high conflict near the cell and the market reduce local GDP; GDP is higher near mines; GDP tends to increase with population size; and there is an increasing but concave relationship between agricultural land suitability (with the potential cassava yield serving as a proxy) and local GDP.

Table B2.2.1 Economic Effects of Transport Cost to Local Market

Dependent variable: Local GDP (2010)	(1) OLS	(2) 2SLS
ln(Cost to market)	−0.016***	−0.046***
	(0.0047)	(0.012)
Indicator: high conflict cell	0.020***	0.250***
	(0.0072)	(0.079)
Indicator: high conflict market	−0.023***	−0.175***
	(0.0066)	(0.02)
ln(Distance to nearest mine)	−0.067***	−0.024***
	(0.006)	(0.0094)
ln(Population)	0.528***	0.528***
	(0.0031)	(0.0032)
ln(Population)^2	0.036***	0.036***
	(0.00027)	(0.00029)
ln(Cassava potential yield)	0.240***	0.197***
	(0.03)	(0.04)
ln(Cassava potential yield)^2	−0.019***	−0.016***
	(0.0026)	(0.0028)
Number of observations	26,535	25,523

Note: Standard errors in parentheses. 2SLS = two-stage least squares; OLS = ordinary least squares.
Significance level: * = 10 percent, ** = 5 percent, *** = 1 percent.

others (2015) also show that in the Democratic Republic of Congo, reducing transport costs could have a significant, positive impact on wealth accumulation and poverty reduction.

Road transport costs could be reduced in several ways. The most obvious, and likely the most costly way, would be to build new roads and bridges. In the context of the major urban center road network proposal, new road construction is a very small part of the overall project. Although some vital portions of the road network are missing, much of the network is already in place. Instead of new construction, much of the network will need to be improved from poor or fair condition to good condition. According to the Highway Development and Management Model used in this analysis, transforming a road from poor to good condition could reduce the cost of traveling along it by nearly 50 percent. Improving it may also ensure that the road is passable all year round, and not just in the dry season, the benefit from which is not quantified by this model.

Concluding Remarks

The analysis above highlights several key points. The current road network is insufficient for long-distance travel throughout the Democratic Republic of Congo. For travel between Kinshasa and most parts of the country, a multimodal approach that uses both roads and rivers is often necessary. For transport to local markets, the optimal route typically only uses roads; river transport would rarely be used. Two projects are proposed. The first focuses on improving access to ports to improve long-distance transport in the short term. Recognizing that relying solely on the river for transport is not a sustainable, long-term solution, another project is proposed to connect major urban centers with Kinshasa using a fully integrated road network. Chapter 4 revisits this project and, using the results of the regression analysis performed in this chapter, estimates the economic benefits of such a project.

Notes

1. Note that the analysis assumes that 1 ton of goods is shipped in a large truck or river barge. If more or fewer goods are shipped, the cost would change accordingly. However, it is not the actual cost that is important for this analysis, but the relative costs between different locations, so this assumption is made merely for comparative purposes.

2. When considering the road network leading to ports, some roads will be more important than others. Improving those that serve the most people is likely to have the biggest impact in the short term by not only improving connectivity to the local markets where the ports are located but also to Kinshasa via the multimodal network. These roads were identified by calculating the optimal road for getting to the nearest port for each portion of the country, and selecting the sections of road from the country's network that have the potential to be traversed by the

largest population. When determining the number of people served by each road or port, the model assumes that all residents are equally likely to transport goods. Without information on who is most likely to use the roads—data that in all likelihood do not exist—assuming uniform road usage is necessary.

References

Ali, R., A. F. Barra, C. N. Berg, R. Damania, J. D. Nash, and J. Russ. 2015. "Infrastructure in Conflict-Prone and Fragile Environments: Evidence from the Democratic Republic of Congo." Policy Research Working Paper 7273, World Bank, Washington, DC.

Ghosh, T., R. L. Powell, C. D. Elvidge, K. E. Baugh, P. C. Sutton, and S. Anderson. 2010. "Shedding Light on the Global Distribution of Economic Activity." *Open Geography Journal* 3 (1): 148–61.

World Bank. 2014. "Democratic Republic of the Congo River and Urban Transport Review." Report ACS9800, World Bank, Washington, DC.

CHAPTER 3

Roads, Forests, and the Biodiversity of the Democratic Republic of Congo

Motivation

The Democratic Republic of Congo, the largest country in Sub-Saharan Africa, is endowed with the second-largest rain forests in the world. The iconic Congo forests are a trove of economic value—some monetizable and much that is not. The forests of the Congo Basin are home to about 30 million people from more than 100 ethnic groups, and remain a crucial livelihood asset, often generating more income for the poor than that obtained from farming (Angelsen and others 2014). Forests also perform valuable ecological services at local, regional, and global levels. Local and regional services include maintenance of the hydrological cycle and important flood control in a high-rainfall region. The forests harbor between 30 and 40 gigatons of carbon, which is equal to 8 percent of the world's forest carbon, the equivalent of three to five years of world emissions of carbon dioxide equivalent.

The carbon sequestered by the forests gives the Democratic Republic of Congo the potential to leverage considerable financial resources being made available through the Reducing Emissions from Deforestation and Forest Degradation (REDD+) initiative. The initial national program in the country, which helped launch and structure the nationwide REDD+ strategy, has transitioned into the full National Program (Readiness Plan). When fully implemented, REDD+ has the potential to create new opportunities that provide incentives for improved stewardship of the forests and the carbon that they sequester and as a consequence innumerable other benefits such as climate regulation, livelihood support, and biodiversity protection.

The Democratic Republic of Congo has the resources and potential to become one of the richest countries in the region. The country's comparative advantage clearly derives from its immense endowment of natural resources—forests, minerals, and water resources. Prudent economic management therefore calls for proper stewardship of these natural assets to ensure sustainable and equitable economic growth. However, harnessing the growth potential of these endowments is not without challenges. It calls for carefully weighing the country's natural capital and the services it provides against other potential land uses. One of the greatest challenges for the Democratic Republic of Congo is to determine the location of roads. As noted in chapter 1, the country's transport infrastructure is severely deficient even by the standards of other low-income countries. It is therefore no surprise that road construction and rehabilitation remains a high priority for both the government of the Democratic Republic of Congo and its major development partners.

However, although roads may bring benefits and are vital for commercializing agriculture, they are often also the precursors to deforestation. A common response to such threats is the creation of protected areas that prevent or severely restrict intrusive structures within demarcated areas. Often, such strategies fail to protect critical natural assets for several reasons. First, governments may seek to minimize economic opportunity costs by siting protected areas in remote regions with low agricultural potential that may not coincide with the areas of highest ecological value (such as climate regulation, biodiversity, or watershed benefits). Second, attempts to restrict road improvements in protected areas with strong agricultural or mineral potential may fail because economic interests invariably overwhelm the limited resources of conservation interests. The vast literature on the political economy of environmental policy suggests two reasons for this outcome. First, the benefits of land conversion are concentrated, while the environmental costs are diffused. Collective action problems render lobbying by environmental groups more difficult. Second, the benefits from land conversion are monetary, while the costs are typically nonpecuniary and emerge in the future, creating a further asymmetry in bargaining ability. The result is higher levels of land conversion and environmental loss than may be either economically optimal or desired by constituencies.

Approach

This chapter seeks to mitigate such conflicts by developing a high-resolution spatial econometric model of road improvement impacts that includes both ecological risks and the economics of forest clearing. The objective is to provide a methodology for prospective assessments that can inform infrastructure planning at the outset. By understanding impacts (positive or otherwise) of a road or other infrastructure, better decisions can be made about ways to locate roads that maximize benefits and minimize costs. The focus of this chapter is on the physical impacts of roads on forests, the previous chapter having dealt with the monetary benefits. No attempt is made to value environmental services in large measure because of the high imprecision of estimates and also because there is little consensus on the validity of approaches used to assign a value to important, unmarketed services provided by the ecosystem.

To guide the empirical analysis, a theoretical model of land use change is developed (see annex 3A). The analysis provides a key insight. Typically, decisions about road improvement projects are made sequentially. Once the location of a road is determined, an environmental impact assessment (EIA) follows that attempts to identify where forests may be cleared and to mitigate the resulting impacts by strengthening environmental management. The analysis shows why infrastructure planning in such a sequential decision regime may actually reduce welfare because it increases deforestation and the associated ecological and social impacts beyond what is economically optimal. The model, together with a body of empirical evidence, suggests that such reactive approaches are inadequate in situations encountered in the Democratic Republic of Congo and will influence outcomes less effectively. Instead, siting decisions and impacts need to be considered simultaneously.

Put simply, the sequencing needs to be altered. The EIA process needs to occur in conjunction with siting plans. Such upstream planning has been rendered both feasible and cost-effective with the availability of georeferenced information on forest cover and economic data. This chapter provides the data and easily comprehensible maps for such an exercise. The maps provide simple visual tools that summarize a computationally intensive exercise. Chapter 4 demonstrates a procedure for identifying hazards, win-wins, and areas where difficult trade-offs may need to occur. The data made available as a result of this exercise could provide valuable information for policies such as REDD+ prioritization, the location of growth poles, agricultural zones, and so on. The data and approach are perhaps timely and valuable given that much development and the need for determining trade-offs is likely to occur in the next few decades.

Results on Forest Clearing

The assessment begins by mapping changes in forest cover and correlating these changes with geographic and socioeconomic variables. The analysis uses the most recent and comprehensive high-resolution data on forest cover from Hansen and others (2013). The data are available at a 30 meter spatial resolution for 2000–12 and are converted for tractability into 2.7 kilometer grid cells. The econometric estimates are remarkably robust and stable across different statistical specifications in the regressions. Details are provided in annex 3B.

The results suggest that forest clearing intensity declines on average with (a) distance from roads, (b) closeness to protected areas, and (c) less accessible terrain (for example, higher elevation). It increases on average with (d) improvements in road conditions, (e) the agricultural value of land (opportunity cost), (f) closeness to population agglomerations (that is, urban centers), and (g) conflict intensity.

Figure 3.1 illustrates two noteworthy patterns. First, upgrading roads from very poor to good condition produces near-complete deforestation within a narrow corridor (of about 1–1.5 kilometer radius) straddling the road.

Figure 3.1 Effect of Road Quality on Forest Clearing Intensity

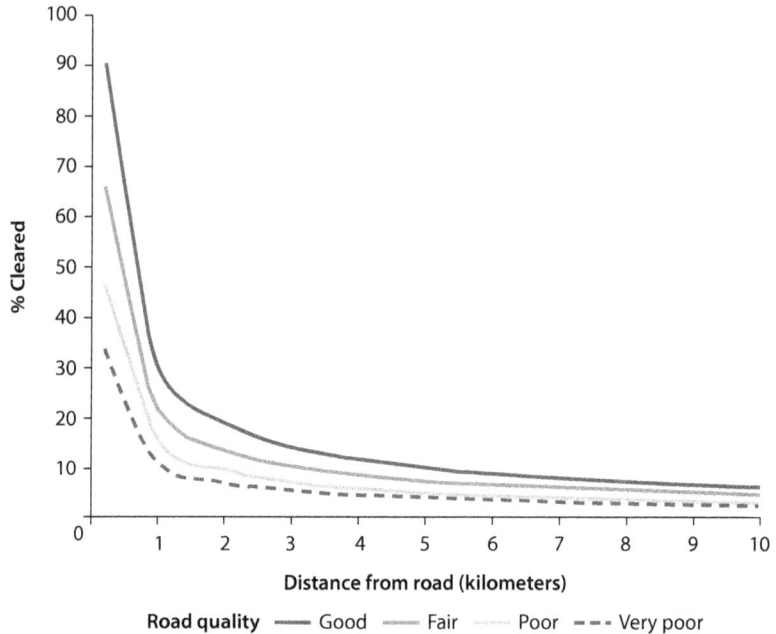

Second, the impact is nonlinear and deforestation intensity falls very rapidly as distance from the road increases. Most of the deforestation occurs within about a 2 kilometer radius of the road. This knowledge may be a useful result for planning and siting roads in areas of high ecological sensitivity. It suggests that a relatively small detour may be sufficient to protect important natural assets.

Map 3.1 applies the analysis to the eastern portion of the Democratic Republic of Congo and provides an illustration of the extent of clearing that might occur with road upgrading. Panel a shows current deforestation (percent cleared) along the major existing roads. Panel b performs a hypothetical experiment whereby all of the roads are improved from their current state to "good" condition. Factors such as current road condition, distance from urban center, and elevation determine the intensity of clearing and the eventual amount of forest cover along any segment. Increases in deforestation of 10–20 percent are typical, with significant extensions of deforested territory along many corridors depending upon local circumstances. Intensive clearing is more pervasive nearer urban centers (where population density and economic activity are concentrated) and in relatively narrow corridors.

Map 3.2 extends the analysis across the country. It is meant to be illustrative and displays changes in mean deforestation rates produced by road upgrading to good condition that would allow vehicle speeds of about 60 kilometers per hour. Note, however, that these spatial averages conceal very wide variations within each cluster.

Map 3.1 Eastern Democratic Republic of Congo: Change in Percent Clearing along Roads without and with Upgrading

a. Clearing along roads without upgrading

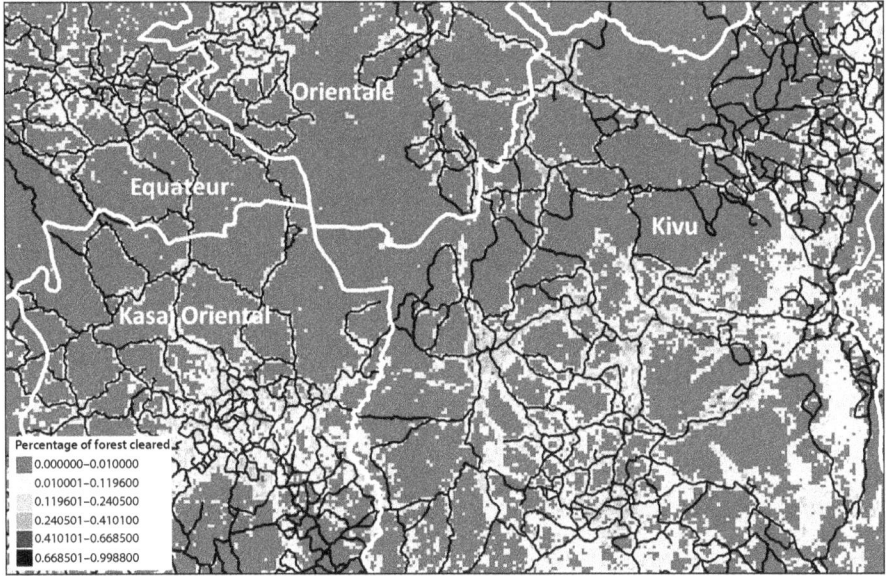

Percentage of forest cleared
- 0.000000–0.010000
- 0.010001–0.119600
- 0.119601–0.240500
- 0.240501–0.410100
- 0.410101–0.668500
- 0.668501–0.998800

b. Clearing along roads with upgrading

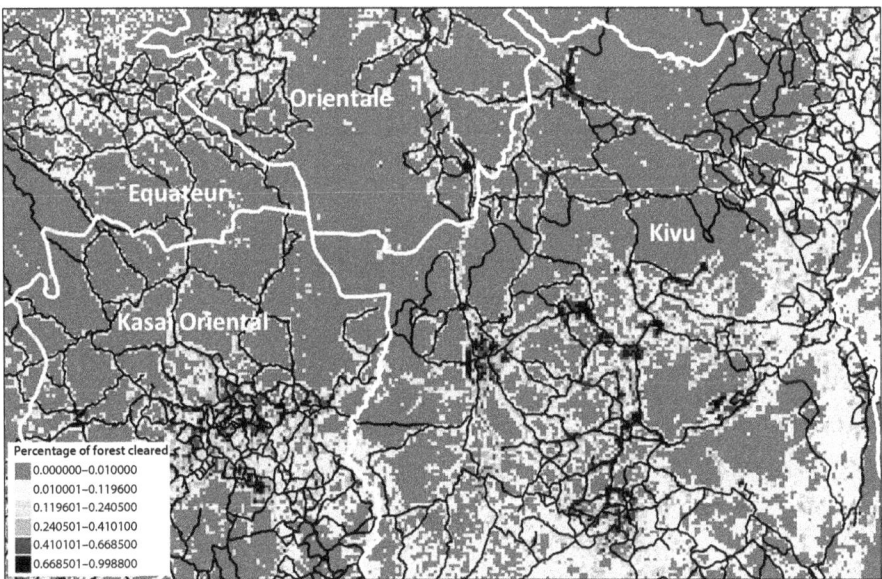

Percentage of forest cleared
- 0.000000–0.010000
- 0.010001–0.119600
- 0.119601–0.240500
- 0.240501–0.410100
- 0.410101–0.668500
- 0.668501–0.998800

Map 3.2 Changes in Road Corridor Deforestation with Generalized Upgrading

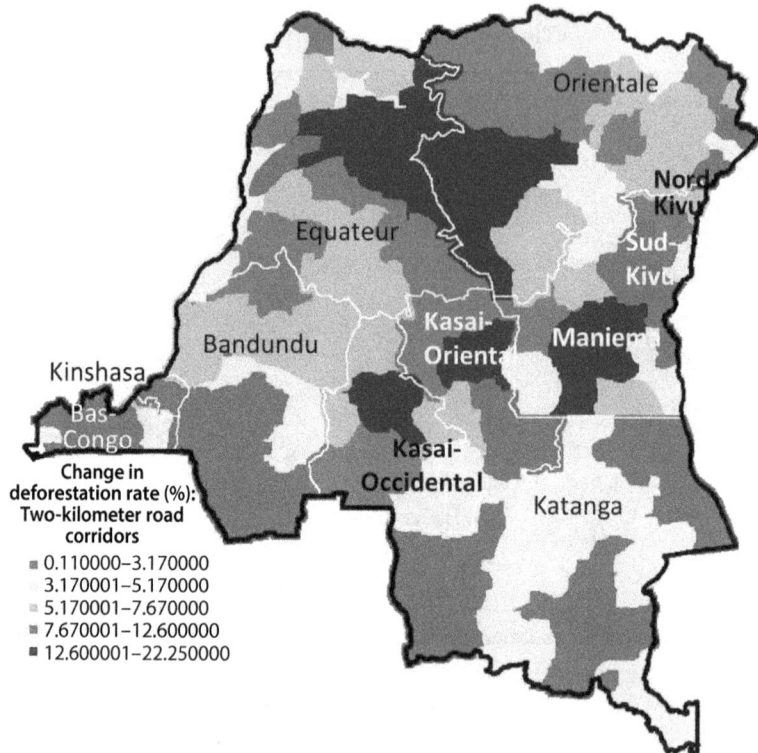

The heaviest impacts (increases of 12.6–22.3 percent) are evident in west Orientale, east Equateur, central Kasai-Occidental, northeast Kasai-Oriental, and central Maniema. Adjacent areas in all five provinces also have significant impacts (7.7–12.6 percent). The greatest impacts are concentrated in relatively isolated rain forest areas with poor roads, since market access for these areas would be most improved by upgrading. Overall, the results indicate that 10–20 percent increases in deforestation would be common after upgrading in rain forest road corridors.

Gradients of Biodiversity Impacts

Not all forest land is of uniform ecological value, nor is it of uniform economic value. This section develops a variety of metrics to identify areas that are of high ecological value and at higher risk of degradation. Spatial analysis of carbon stocks in the Democratic Republic of Congo and of biodiversity habitats has largely confirmed that there are significant overlaps: areas that store large amounts of biomass carbon may coincide with areas of biodiversity significance (Musampa Kaungandu and others 2012). An opportunity therefore arises to realize and monetize many of these multiple benefits through the REDD+ process.

This correlation suggests that it is important for the country to identify and appropriately manage areas that generate multiple gains to maximize both the monetary and nonmonetary benefits from the forests.

Efforts to develop a single index of ecological value remain elusive and beset with difficulties of enumeration and measurement. Nor is there a consensus on the weighting of different risks and species. To address these issues, this study develops a "gradient approach" that combines information on species as well as ecosystems. This approach has practical policy merit. Some road corridors will be built in areas of modest ecological concern, whereas others pass through areas of higher value. An ecological gradient strategy can be used to minimize ecological damage by favoring road improvements in areas of modest concentration.[1]

The biodiversity gradient has several components. Species density provides critical information for developing ecogradients, but at least three other elements are needed:

- First is *geographic vulnerability*, for which endemicity can serve as a proxy. Species that reside in very few grid cells may be particularly vulnerable to habitat encroachment.
- Second, *extinction risk* adds the insights of the international scientific community. Work by Mooers, Faith, and Maddison (2008) explicitly models the relationship between extinction probability and the risk indicator that is provided for each species by the International Union for Conservation of Nature (IUCN).[2]
- Third, other aspects of the ecosystem as captured through a *measure of biomes* developed by the World Wildlife Fund (WWF) are incorporated.

Endemicity is measured by the percentage of each species' range that is found in each grid cell. Total endemicity for each grid cell—the sum of its species endemicity measures—assigns higher values to cells inhabited by species whose ranges are relatively limited. By implication, forest clearing in higher-value cells may be particularly destructive for remaining critical habitat. Species differ in vulnerability for many reasons that are not captured by the endemicity measure. To incorporate these factors, the threat status code assigned to each species by the IUCN is used along with extinction probabilities estimated using the methodology of Mooers, Faith, and Maddison (2008). Table 3.1 tabulates conversions from Red List codes[3] to normalized species weights using four probability assignments. Three of these probability assignments use IUCN estimates to derive measures of extinction probability over the next 50, 100, and 500 years. The fourth draws on work by Isaac and others (2007), who combine a direct extinction risk measure with a measure of each species' isolation on a phylogenetic tree.[4] Each measure provides different priorities and information. For instance, a spatial grid containing very diverse species, all in the "Least concern" category, would be given a relatively low weight by the IUCN measure. But by the Isaacs measure, it would be deemed more important because of the elevated genetic diversity of species, even when none are critically endangered.

Table 3.1 Normalized Species Aggregation Weight

		Normalized extinction probabilities			
		Isaac and others 2007[a]	IUCN: future years		
IUCN Code	Status		50	100	500
CR	Critically endangered	1.00000	1.00000	1.00000	1.00000
EN	Endangered	0.50000	0.43299	0.66770	0.99600
VU	Vulnerable	0.25000	0.05155	0.10010	0.39000
NT	Near threatened	0.12500	0.00412	0.01000	0.02000
LC	Least concern	0.06250	0.00005	0.00010	0.00050
	Rounded weight ratios				
	CR:EN	2	2	1	1
	CR:VU	4	19	10	3
	CR:NT	8	243	100	50
	CR:LC	16	20,000	10,000	2,000

Source: Data from Mooers, Faith, and Maddison 2008.
Note: IUCN = International Conservation of Nature.
a. From calculations by Mooers, Faith, and Maddison (2008) based on Isaac and others (2007).

An ecogradient measure based on species vulnerability alone provides an incomplete accounting of ecological values and functions. A more comprehensive measure would need to incorporate biomes. Using the WWF classification of ecoregions,[5] a vulnerability index is derived that measures the amount of an ecoregion in a given area. The WWF ecoregions serve as a general proxy for distinctive plant, insect, and animal species that are not represented in the range maps provided by IUCN and BirdLife International.[6]

Each index generates a different set of priorities. A cautious approach is applied whereby the indicator that generates the highest threat level is used. The indexes are normalized for comparability using ranks measured as percentiles in each index and selecting the maximum index (risk) value as the ecogradient measure for the cell. This approach gives parity to alternative vulnerability indicators and always picks the indicator that generates the highest threat level.

Map 3.3 combines both sets of information, displaying the distribution of species' ecoregion indexes in the Congo Basin countries. (Because species do not reside within national boundaries, the entire region is displayed to show larger patterns.) One striking feature is the blue/green (0–50) band that arcs from northern Cameroon to the eastern Democratic Republic of Congo and back to the southern Democratic Republic of Congo. Another is the prominent clustering of very high values in western Cameroon, along the border between the Republic of Congo and the Democratic Republic of Congo, and along the eastern margin of the basin. Finally, there are the highly vulnerable "red strips" that identify the habitat of critically endangered species.

For the purposes of this chapter, the most important message in the results is the striking nonuniformity of ecological vulnerability across forested areas. By implication, a full assessment of the benefits and costs of road upgrading should go beyond simple measurement of forest loss to encompass the potential impact of that loss on biological diversity.

The Stakes for Vulnerable Areas

This section joins the strands by combining predicted deforestation from road upgrading with the indexes of ecological vulnerability from map 3.3. The multiple determinants of forest clearing (as discussed in the section title "Results on Forest Clearing") can produce highly varied patterns of road corridor deforestation within the same region. Even more variety emerges when the vulnerability index is included, because the correlation between the measures of clearing and ecological vulnerability is close to zero ($\rho = -0.0356$).

The remaining task of this subsection is simplification, given that combining the two indicators produces results for thousands of road segments. The focus is on communicating the general tenor of results by concentrating on the four-province area featured in map 3.1.

Map 3.3 Composite Species-Ecoregion Index, Congo Basin Countries

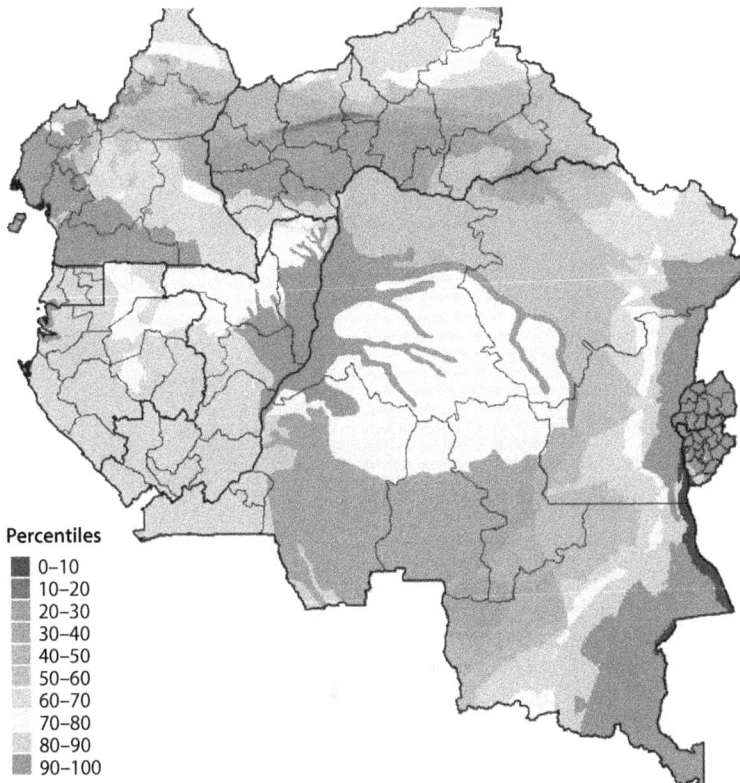

Percentiles
- 0–10
- 10–20
- 20–30
- 30–40
- 40–50
- 50–60
- 60–70
- 70–80
- 80–90
- 90–100

Note: Percentiles show the relative composite species-ecoregion index.

Map 3.4 provides an illustration by overlaying the road network on a composite vulnerability map for four provinces (Kivu, Orientale, Equateur, Kasai Oriental). This high resolution map could be used as a preliminary tool for identifying emerging hotspots of concern, including where REDD+ opportunities may be high, as well as areas where effects of developing new infrastructure would be minimal. This map provides an immediate sense of potential opportunity and vulnerability at different points in a network. Map 3.4 identifies ecological vulnerability in the provinces of concern. As an example, the red zones identify critical habitats for some of the country's endangered primates.

Map 3.5 displays the combined impact indicator, which is the product of the predicted percentage of deforestation from upgrading (map 3.2) and the vulnerability index (map 3.4). The indicator is standardized so that its range is 0–100. To discern the effect of combining the two indicators, compare maps 3.2 and 3.5 for the dense road cluster south of the Kasai Oriental label. In map 3.5, the southern and western parts of the cluster are dominated by indicator scores in the range 0–10 (yellow), whereas the central and eastern parts have clusters in the range 30–100 (red). In part, this pattern reflects variation in biodiversity vulnerability, which is relatively low (green) in the southern part of the cluster and significantly

Map 3.4 Eastern Democratic Republic of Congo—Ecological Vulnerability Map (spatially aggregated)

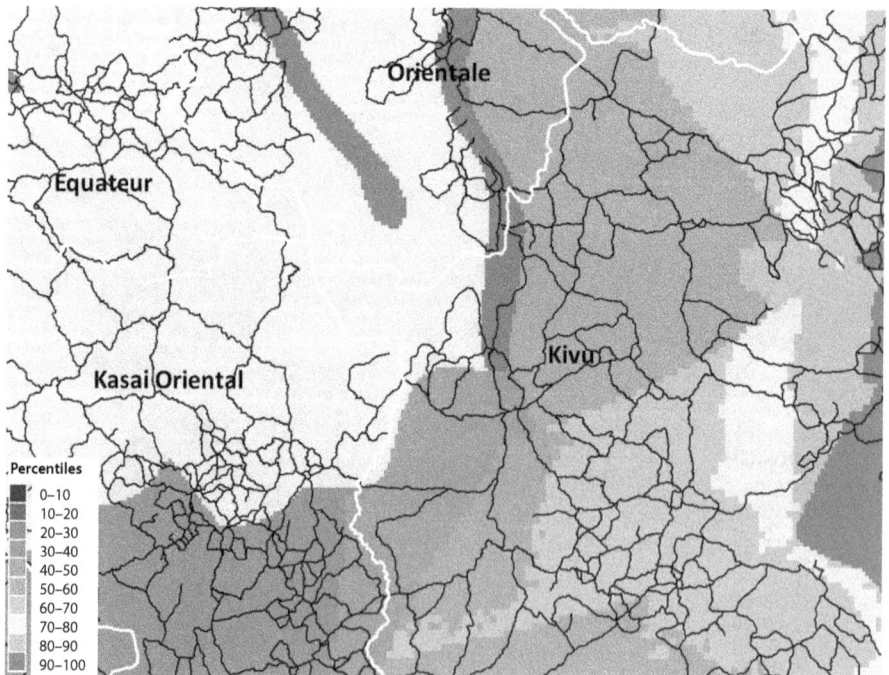

Note: Percentiles show the relative composite species-ecoregion index.

Map 3.5   Combined Ecological Risk from Road Network Improvement in Eastern Democratic Republic of Congo

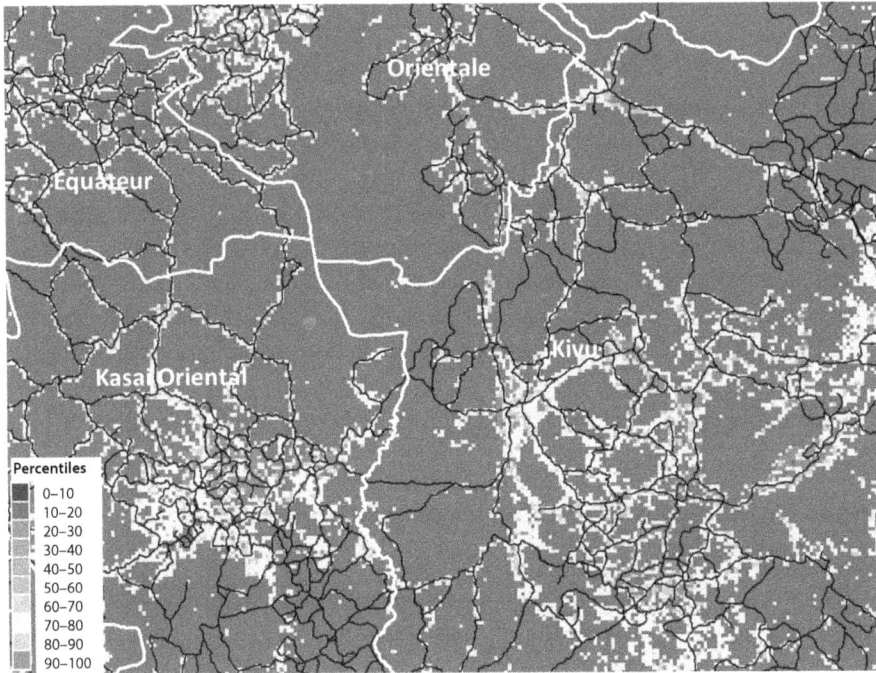

Note: Percentiles show the combined impact indicator, which is the product of the predicted percentage deforestation from upgrading (map 3.2) and the vulnerability index (map 3.4). Indicator is standardized between 0 and 100.

higher (yellow) in the northern part. In conclusion, map 3.5 provides a visual and easy-to-comprehend assessment of vulnerability and risk that can be used for preemptive planning and policy making. An illustration is provided in chapter 4.

Concluding Remarks

This chapter illustrates a method for combining cutting-edge econometrics with conservation biology and generates risk and vulnerability maps that are arguably vitally important for informing the Democratic Republic of Congo's planning process. Overall, the results suggest that the siting of infrastructure needs to consider potential effects on the local forest and ecology at the very outset of the planning process. Sequential decision making, wherein location decisions occur first, followed by an EIA, can lead to economically less favorable outcomes that can be avoided through careful upstream planning. Both new data and new techniques are now available that can be used to identify areas of opportunity, risk, and potential for REDD+ financing.

Using the best available data and robust econometric techniques, this chapter finds large and highly significant effects of road upgrading on the intensity and extent of forest clearing in road corridors. Predicted effects in road corridors vary widely with previous road conditions and locational economics, but increases in deforestation of 10–20 percent are typical.

A high-resolution map of ecological vulnerability is developed. Overlaying the Congo Basin–wide road network on this map provides a first-order guide for risk assessment. Predicted deforestation is uncorrelated with the vulnerability indicator, so the variation in the two separate indicators is compounded in the combined measure. The implications for "smart" infrastructure location are suggested by the maps.

Overall, the results cast doubt on the utility of broad generalizations about the impact of road upgrading on deforestation and biomes. The high-resolution spatial assessment finds impacts as varied as the economic and ecological conditions that prevail in different road corridors. By implication, road improvement planning in tropical forest regions is unlikely to maximize welfare unless it anticipates and incorporates such impacts.

The next chapter combines economic potential with ecological impacts.

Annex 3A: Modeling the Economics of Road Improvement and Deforestation

As noted in chapter 1, this research aims to develop an analysis of road upgrading and forest clearing that incorporates both economic and conservation concerns. The objective is to develop a methodology for prospective assessment that can inform infrastructure planning at the outset. To motivate the exercise, the analysis considers the potentially adverse impact of traditional road improvement planning, in which decision making is sequential. Decisions on road improvement projects in an area are made first, followed by an EIA that seeks to mitigate forest clearing by strengthening environmental management rather than affecting the selection of projects. The modeling exercise shows why infrastructure planning in such a sequential decision regime, while otherwise desirable for its direct economic contribution, may actually reduce welfare because it increases deforestation and the associated ecological impacts.

Consider two regions, labeled i and j, that sell their produce at a market at given distances d_i and d_j, respectively. Each region is endowed with a given amount of land that can either be left forested, or converted to some alternative use such as agriculture, whose outputs are transported to the market and sold at a given price. Let $L_i = L_i^F + L_i^A$ be the total endowment of land in region i, where L_i^F is forested land and L_i^A is agricultural land. The payoffs in region i to each activity are given by

$$\Pi_i = \left(P_i - d_i\left(1 - q_i\right)\right)L_i^A - c_i L_i^{A^2} + v\left(L_i - L_i^A\right),   \text{(3A.1)}$$

in which P_i is the exogenous market price and $0 \le q_i < 1$ is an index of road quality, with $q = 0$ representing an unimproved forest track. Improvements in road quality (q) lower transport costs and increase the profitability of agricultural production. With convex costs, returns to forest conversion are assumed to be diminishing $(c_i L_i^{A^2})$. Finally, forests left in their natural state generate a return of v, which could include livelihood and other unmarketed benefits obtained from the forest.

Maximizing equation (3A.1), taking road quality as given, yields the optimal level of clearing (output) in region i:

$$L_i^A = \frac{p_i - d_i(1 - q_i)}{2c_i}, \qquad (3A.2)$$

in which $p_i = P_i + v$. The corresponding indirect profit function from the land use decision is

$$\Pi_i = \frac{(p_i - d_i(1 - q_i))^2}{4c_i} + vL_i. \qquad (3A.3)$$

Region j is symmetric and its specification is suppressed for brevity. It is clear from equation (3A.3) that higher market prices or improvements in road quality lead to greater land conversion $\left(\text{that is,} \frac{\partial L_i^A}{\partial dq_i} = \frac{d_i}{2c_i} > 0 \text{ and } \frac{\partial L_i^A}{\partial dp_i} = \frac{1}{2c_i} > 0 \right)$. This straightforward result reflects the fact that higher profitability of agriculture or increased market access renders deforestation and land conversion more profitable. The less well known question is how these incentives might vary under different decision-making regimes. The following discussion compares deforestation levels in each region under two contrasting forms of management. In the first, the decision on road quality improvements is made autonomously in each jurisdiction. In the alternative, the budget allocation is coordinated to maximize the joint welfare of the two regions. The discussion assumes that environmental impacts are not considered in the decision-making process.[7]

Consider first the case of autonomous decision making. For simplicity assume that there is a fixed budget B_i available for road quality improvements in region i. The cost of improving road quality is given by $B_i = rd_i q_i$. If the budget constraint binds, then road quality is given by

$$q_i^I = \frac{B_i}{rd_i}. \qquad (3A.4)$$

Thus, road quality declines with distance (d_i) and the costs of road construction (r). Substituting in equation (3A.2), the amount of land conversion is

$$L_i^A = \frac{p_i - d_i\left(1 - \dfrac{B_i}{rd_i}\right)}{2c_i}. \qquad (3A.5)$$

In contrast, under coordinated management the budget is allocated to maximize the joint welfare of the two regions:

$$Max \; W = \frac{(p_i - d_i(1 - q_i))^2}{4c_i} + vL_i + \frac{(p_j - d_j(1 - q_j))^2}{4c_j} + vL_j$$

$$\text{subject to } B_i - rd_i q_i - rd_j q_j, \tag{3A.6}$$

which yields solutions for the optimal improvements in road quality:

$$q_i^c = \frac{c_i B_i + r\left(c_i \theta_j - c_j \theta_i\right)}{rd_i\left(c_i + c_j\right)} \text{ and } q_j^c = \frac{c_j B_j + r\left(c_j \theta_i - c_i \theta_j\right)}{rd_j\left(c_i + c_j\right)}, \tag{3A.7}$$

in which $\theta_k = p_k - d_k$, for $(k = i, j)$.

For later use it is instructive to observe that $\dfrac{\partial q_i}{\partial c_i} = \dfrac{\left(c_j B_i + rc_j\left(\theta_i + \theta_j\right)\right)}{rd_i(rc_{i} + c_j)^2} > 0.$

As land conversion costs rise in a region, road quality is improved. Intuitively, road investments are made to equate the marginal payoffs from agricultural sales from each region. With diminishing returns to land conversion, it eventually pays to invest in the higher-cost region. The following lemmas compare road investments and deforestation rates under the different regimes:

Lemma 1. If the cost of land conversion between regions differs sufficiently, then road improvements in the high-cost region will be greater under coordinated management than under autonomous management $\left(\text{that is, } q_i^l < q_i^c \text{ if } \dfrac{c_i}{c_j} > \dfrac{(B_i + 2r\,\theta_i)}{(B_i + 2r\,\theta_j)}\right).$

Intuitively, under autonomous management, budgets available to each region are fixed, whereas under coordinated management the region with the higher costs of land conversion could receive a higher allocation to equalize marginal payoffs. An implication of this result is that total deforestation rates may differ across management regimes. This result is summarized in Lemma 2 and illustrated in figure 3A.1.

Lemma 2. Total deforestation rates will differ under the management regimes and will be higher under coordinated management if the cost of land conversion is sufficiently large in one of the regions $\left(\text{that is, } q_i^l + q_j^l < q_i^c + q_j^c \text{ if } c_i > \dfrac{c_j(B_i + 2r\,\theta_i)}{(B_i + 2r\,\theta_j)}\right).$

When differences between regions are large, under coordinated management, total payoffs are maximized by ensuring that the region with the comparative advantage in land clearing receives greater support on the margin, thus expanding the total volume of land cleared. This result follows from the convex cost of land conversion, which implies that the incremental returns to further deforestation will be lower in the region with a sufficiently high level of land conversion. Figure 3A.1 illustrates this relationship—as costs in region i rise, it receives improved road quality and as a result incurs higher rates of deforestation and ecological losses. By implication, coordinated regional infrastructure planning, while promoted for its economic benefits, may actually increase deforestation in a sequential decision regime that selects road projects first and introduces environmental impact analysis afterward. As an alternative, the approach developed in this paper seeks to improve the decision process by enabling simultaneous consideration of potential road projects and deforestation impacts.

Figure 3A.1 Road Planning Regimes, Road Quality, and Deforestation

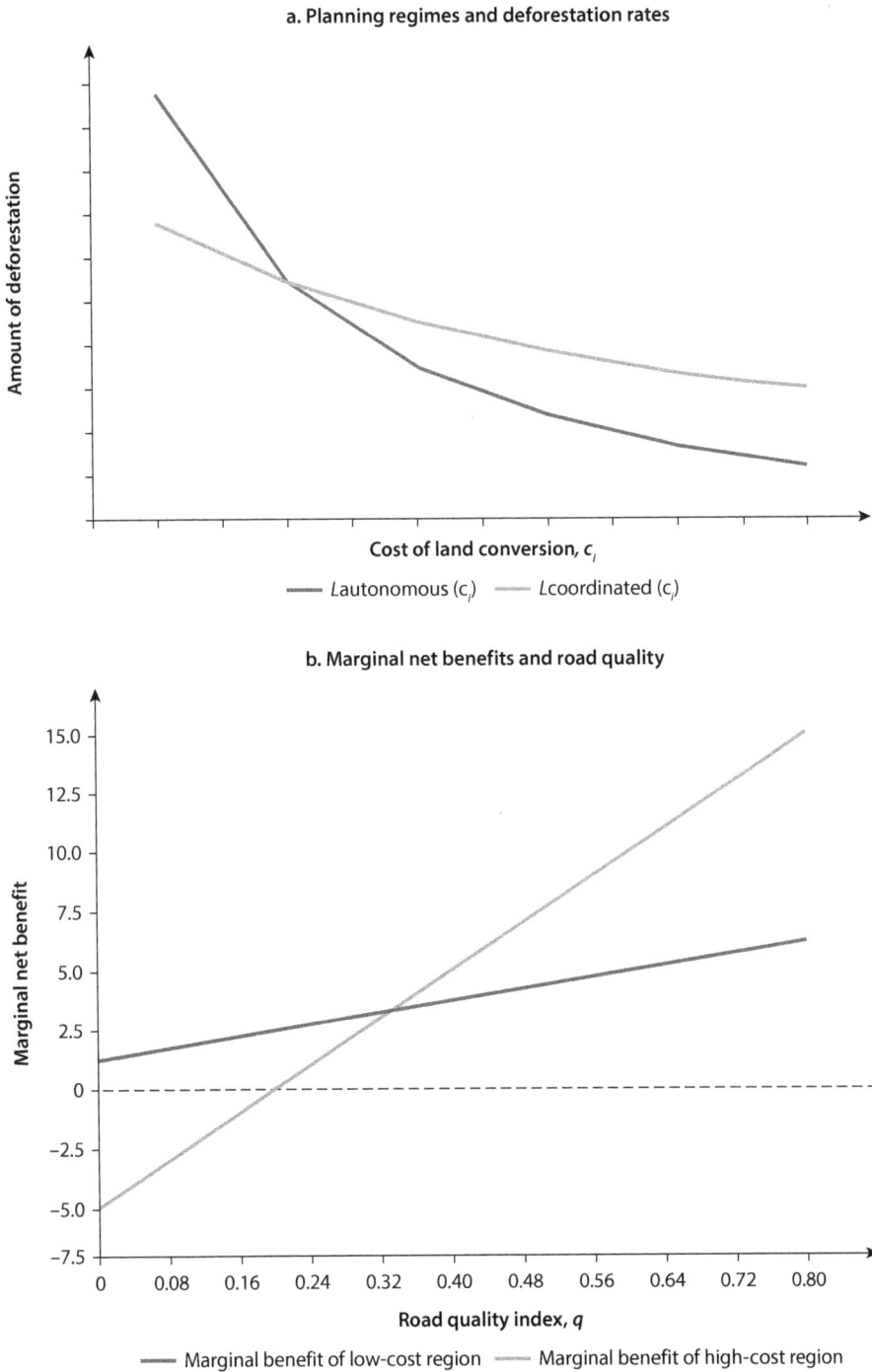

a. Planning regimes and deforestation rates

Cost of land conversion, c_i

— Lautonomous (c_i)   ⋯ Lcoordinated (c_i)

b. Marginal net benefits and road quality

— Marginal benefit of low-cost region   ⋯ Marginal benefit of high-cost region

Annex 3B: Econometric Results

Table 3B.1 Regression Results for the Democratic Republic of Congo (all nondummy variables in log form)

	(1) OLS	(2) OLS	(3) 2SLS	(4) GLS (IV)	(5) Robust (IV)
Distance from road	−0.298	−0.309	−0.309	−0.309	−0.296
	(29.97)**	(30.43)**	(30.43)**	(8.80)**	(32.77)**
Protected area × Distance from road	−0.165	−0.204	−0.204	−0.204	−0.152
	(18.56)**	(22.79)**	(22.79)**	(2.91)**	(19.18)**
Road condition	0.544	0.455	0.455	0.455	0.513
	(17.56)**	(13.76)**	(13.76)**	(1.57)	(17.49)**
Transport cost to nearest urban center	−0.481		−0.952	−0.952	−0.876
	(34.15)**		(23.54)**	(3.28)**	(24.39)**
Euclidean distance to nearest urban center		−0.279			
		(23.54)**			
Land opportunity value	−0.091	−0.023	−0.023	−0.023	0.004
	(10.32)**	(2.63)**	(2.63)**	(0.37)	(0.46)
Elevation	−0.066	−0.130	−0.130	−0.130	−0.238
	(2.06)*	(3.97)**	(3.97)**	(0.59)	(8.18)**
Conflict intensity (1997–2007)	0.016	0.029	0.029	0.029	−0.000
	(5.52)**	(9.96)**	(9.96)**	(1.23)	(0.10)
D2002	0.935	0.934	0.934	0.934	0.925
	(21.93)**	(21.46)**	(21.46)**	(19.61)**	(23.92)**
D2003	1.269	1.269	1.269	1.269	1.246
	(29.78)**	(29.15)**	(29.15)**	(22.76)**	(32.24)**
D2004	1.559	1.558	1.558	1.558	1.542
	(36.58)**	(35.81)**	(35.81)**	(27.75)**	(39.91)**
D2005	1.827	1.826	1.826	1.826	1.810
	(42.87)**	(41.97)**	(41.97)**	(32.71)**	(46.86)**
D2006	1.983	1.982	1.982	1.982	1.972
	(46.56)**	(45.58)**	(45.58)**	(36.81)**	(51.07)**
D2007	2.155	2.154	2.154	2.154	2.145
	(50.59)**	(49.52)**	(49.52)**	(38.55)**	(55.55)**
D2008	2.278	2.278	2.278	2.278	2.271
	(53.50)**	(52.37)**	(52.37)**	(40.65)**	(58.81)**
D2009	2.462	2.462	2.462	2.462	2.456
	(57.81)**	(56.60)**	(56.60)**	(44.19)**	(63.62)**
D2010	2.651	2.650	2.650	2.650	2.647
	(62.25)**	(60.94)**	(60.94)**	(48.34)**	(68.56)**
D2011	2.747	2.746	2.746	2.746	2.738
	(64.50)**	(63.14)**	(63.14)**	(48.95)**	(70.92)**
D2012	2.832	2.831	2.831	2.831	2.821
	(66.48)**	(65.09)**	(65.09)**	(49.73)**	(73.06)**
Constant	4.810	4.806	6.747	6.747	7.255
	(23.39)**	(22.07)**	(25.94)**	(4.07)**	(31.42)**
Observations	13,758	13,758	13,758	13,758	13,758
R-squared	0.49	0.47	0.47	0.47	0.51

Note: Absolute value of *t*-statistics in parentheses. 2SLS = two-stage least squares; GLS = generalized least squares; IV = instrumental variables; OLS = ordinary least squares.
Significance level: * = 5 percent, ** = 1 percent.

Notes

1. A composite gradient is developed that includes measures of endemicity, extinction risk (from the International Union for Conservation of Nature), and phylogenetic significance and extinction probabilities (from Isaac and others 2007). Each index generates a different set of priorities.
2. The IUCN's current classification categories are Critically Endangered, Endangered, Vulnerable, Near Threatened, and Least Concern.
3. Red List codes categorize the threatened status of a species. See: http://www .iucnredlist.org/technical-documents/categories-and-criteria/2001-categories-criteria.
4. A phylogenetic tree is a branching tree diagram that traces the evolutionary descent of different species from a common ancestor. Species in sparse (isolated) branches of a phylogenetic tree are relatively unique, since they share common descent patterns with fewer other species.
5. Defined as "a large unit of land or water containing a geographically distinct assemblage of species, natural communities, and environmental conditions" (http://www .worldwildlife.org/biomes).
6. The method for incorporating WWF ecoregions resembles this study's treatment of species endemicity. For the group of selected countries, the percentage of total area accounted for by each ecoregion is computed. Its vulnerability index is then computed as the inverse of its area share, and the appropriate index value is assigned to each pixel in the Congo Basin countries, where a pixel is a 2.7 kilometer grid cell. This accounting assigns high values to pixels in smaller ecoregions, where clearing single pixels may pose more significant threats to biome integrity.
7. This describes a not-uncommon situation in which decision making is sequential, with decisions on road location made first, followed by an EIA process that typically seeks to mitigate impacts by strengthening environmental management rather than altering road routing.

References

Angelsen, A., Pamela Jagger, Ronnie Babigumira, Brian Belcher, Nicholas J. Hogarth, Simone Bauch, Jan Börner, Carsten Smith-Hall, and Sven Wunder. 2014. "Environmental Income and Rural Livelihoods: A Global-Comparative Analysis." *World Development* 64 (1): S12–28. http://dx.doi.org/10.1016/j.worlddev.2014.03.006.

Hansen, M. C., P. V. Potapov, R. Moore, M. Hancher, S. A. Turubanova, A. Tyukavina, D. Thau, S. V. Stehman, S. J. Goetz, T. R. Loveland, A. Kommareddy, A. Egorov, L. Chini, C. O. Justice, and J. R. G. Townshend. 2013. "High-Resolution Global Maps of 21st-Century Forest Cover Change." *Science* 342 (6160): 850–53.

Isaac, N., S. Turvey, B. Collen, C. Waterman, and J. Baillie. 2007. "Mammals on the EDGE: Conservation Priorities Based on Threat and Phylogeny." *PLoS One* 2: e29.

Mooers, Arne Ø., Daniel Faith, and Wayne Maddison. 2008. "Converting Endangered Species Categories to Probabilities of Extinction for Phylogenetic Conservation Prioritization." *PLoS One* 3 (11): e3700. doi: 10.1371/journal.pone.0003700.

Musampa Kamungandu, C., L. Mane, P. Lola Amani, M. Bertzky, C. Ravilious, M. Osti, L. Miles, V. Kapos, and B. Dickson. 2012. "Mapping Potential Biodiversity Benefits from REDD+. The Democratic Republic of Congo." Prepared by UNEP-WCMC; Ministry of the Environment, Nature Conservation and Tourism of the DRC; and the Satellite Observatory for Central African Forests. UN-REDD Programme, Democratic Republic of Congo.

CHAPTER 4

Economic and Ecological Impact of Prospective Road Investments

Introduction

The previous two chapters demonstrate methodologies that estimate the effects of reducing transport costs by building or improving the road network. Chapter 2 estimates the elasticity of local GDP to a drop in transport costs, and chapter 3 estimates the effects of forest clearing, using Hansen and others (2013) forest data, based on a decline in transport costs. This chapter uses these elasticities in simulations to estimate the potential welfare benefits, as well as deforestation, that would result from the two proposed road investments in the Democratic Republic of Congo.

Although this methodology must be used with due awareness of its shortcomings (described below), it nevertheless provides decision makers with the capability to quantify the potential induced local benefits (increased economic activity) and costs (increased deforestation) of numerous options, and prioritize those that should be evaluated in more depth. This methodology is performed in such a way that it could be applied to study any road improvement or new road construction project within the Democratic Republic of Congo and to prioritize investments.

Two simulations are demonstrated below. The first estimates the benefits, as measured by increased gross domestic product (GDP), and the costs—deforestation and potential biodiversity loss—from the major urban center road network improvement plan introduced in chapter 2. The second simulation estimates the same costs and benefits for a smaller project in the environmentally fragile northeastern part of the country, near Virunga National Park. This theoretical road improvement project involves a road that connects the city of Goma in the province of North Kivu to Bunia, in Orientale province.

Economic Boom or Ecologic Doom? • http://dx.doi.org/10.1596/978-1-4648-0810-4

39

Major Urban Center Road Network Improvement Project

To estimate the impact of improving the quality of a road segment, the primary road network that connects 11 major urban centers with Kinshasa is considered as a prospective project. As shown in chapter 2, map 2.4, the current 6,500 kilometers of roads traverse much of the country, and if in good repair would connect many areas that are currently only linked by river or air travel. It is assumed that this network would be improved from its current quality to "good" condition, with several impassable missing links filled in. In the baseline scenario (current quality), only 20 percent of the network is currently paved, and about 75 percent of the roads are in poor condition.

To calculate the change in transport cost due to the improvement, the same procedure that was used in chapter 2 to estimate travel cost to the cheapest market is followed.[1]

The percentage change in transport costs for each cell if the entire project were completed is shown in map 4.1. Note that the reduction in transport cost to the local market occurs mostly in areas around the improved roads. This is unsurprising because areas that are far from these roads are likely served by markets (if any) that are also far from these roads, and are therefore not affected by the road improvements under consideration.

Estimated Benefits: Increases in Local GDP

The first simulation estimates the increase in local GDP due to the major urban center road network improvement project. Three pieces of data are needed: baseline local GDP, the change in transport costs (to the local market) due to the project, and the elasticity of local GDP to a reduction in local market transport costs. (Chapter 2 provides an explanation of these elasticities, and box 4.1 provides details of how economic benefits are calculated.)

The increase in local GDP is estimated in each grid cell separately, then aggregated to arrive at the total benefit. Map 4.2 shows the spatial distribution of the increase in local GDP.[2] The project is estimated to benefit a large land area around the entire network, with the largest benefits near Bandundu, Goma, and the long stretch of road between Mbandaka and Kisangani. Summing the benefits in all grid cells yields a total annual benefit of US$18.1 million.

The figure of US$18.1 million per year needs to be contextualized. First, this simulation represents a partial equilibrium estimate of the benefits of the road improvement project. If the project leads to significant structural changes in the economy, this methodology would not be a sufficient way to characterize and estimate those changes. Second, it is unlikely that benefits will appear all at once. Rather, benefits will appear gradually, and will likely be layered in over several years. Finally, these benefits are only a subset of the total benefits from reducing transport costs. This model does not include benefits from decreasing transport costs between cities, or between ports. Given that trade between cities (other than Kinshasa) in the Democratic Republic of Congo is currently relatively low, these benefits are also relatively low. Another important caveat to these estimates is that it is not possible to disaggregate economic sectors.

Map 4.1 Change in Transport Costs due to the Major Urban Center Road Network Improvement Project

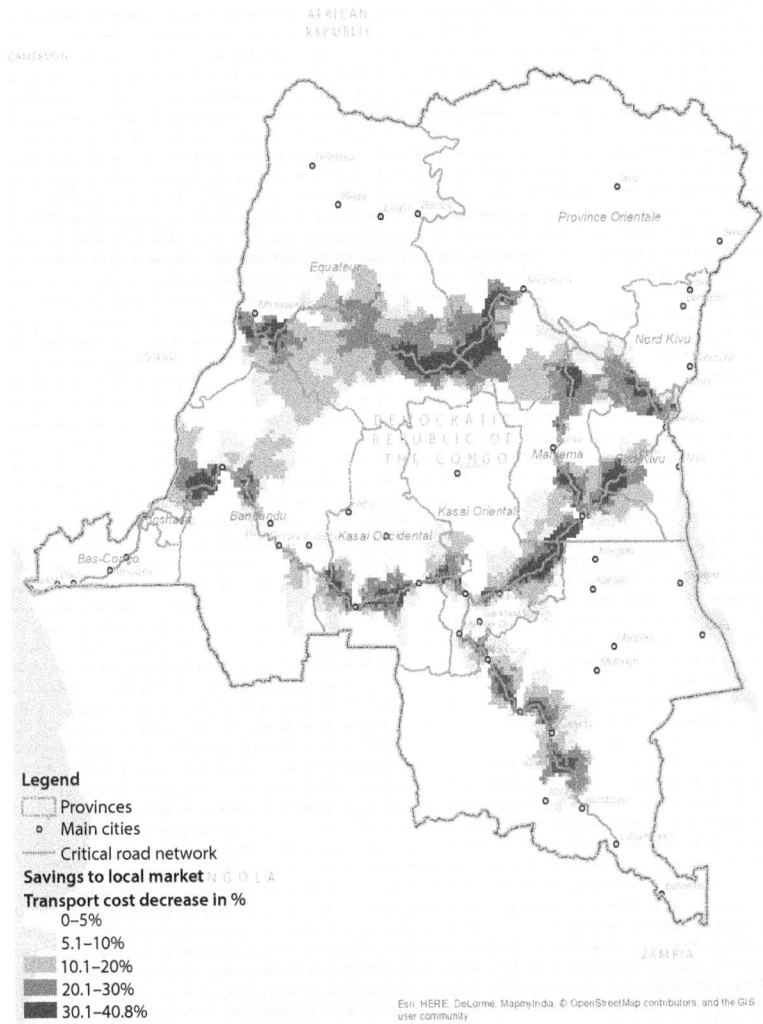

Legend
- Provinces
- o Main cities
- Critical road network

Savings to local market
Transport cost decrease in %
- 0–5%
- 5.1–10%
- 10.1–20%
- 20.1–30%
- 30.1–40.8%

Esri, HERE, DeLorme, MapmyIndia, © OpenStreetMap contributors, and the GIS user community

Note: The map shows the reduction in transport costs to the local market due to the major urban center road network project. Note that in both the baseline case and the with-project case, a unimodal network is assumed where only roads (and thus no rivers) are used for transport.

Box 4.1 Local GDP Simulation

Once the elasticity of local GDP to changes in transport costs is calculated (see chapter 2), simulating the benefits of a reduction in transport costs is straightforward. An elasticity is a measure of one variable's sensitivity to a change in another variable. The elasticity of local GDP to transport cost to the local market, −0.046, implies that a 10 percent decline in transport cost to the local market would increase local GDP by 0.46 percent. This elasticity can therefore be

box continues next page

Box 4.1 Local GDP Simulation (continued)

used to calculate the total increase in local GDP from the major urban center road network improvement project using the following formula:

$$\Delta GDP_i = \eta_M \times \tau_{iM} \times y_i,$$

in which ΔGDP_i is the total increase to local GDP in grid cell i, η_M is local GDP elasticity of transport costs to the local market, τ_{iM} is the percentage change in transport costs to the local market in cell i, and y_i is baseline local GDP in cell i. The total increase in local GDP is then obtained by summing the increases across grid cells.

Map 4.2 Increase in Local GDP from the Major Urban Center Road Network Improvement Project

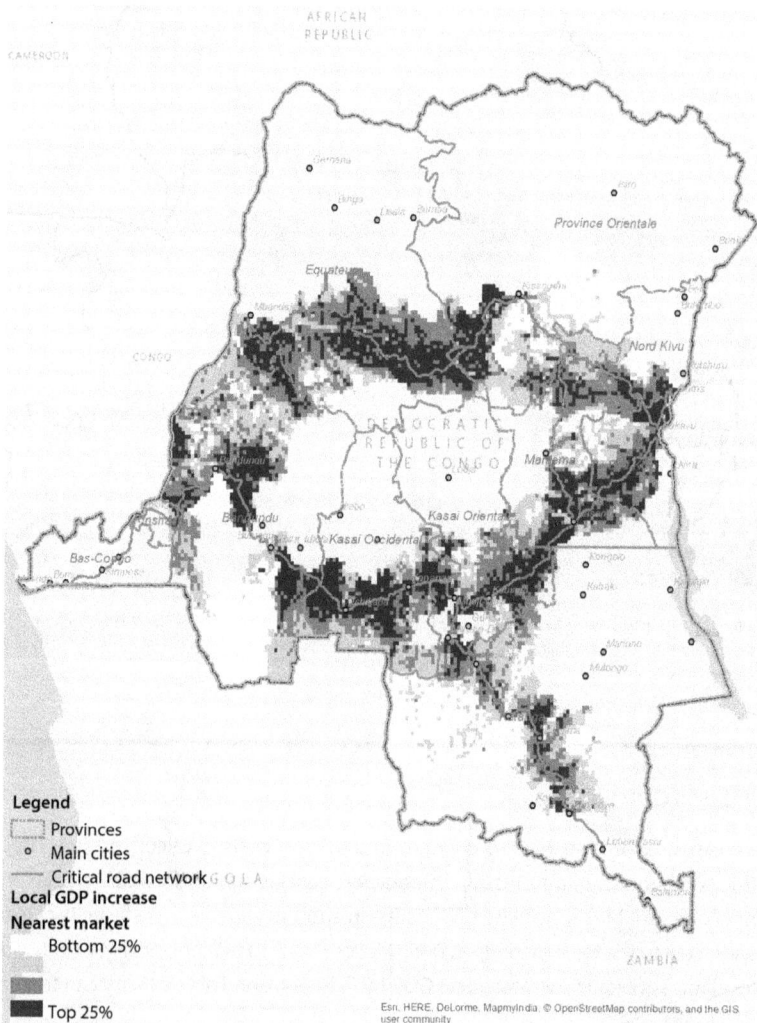

Legend
- Provinces
- ○ Main cities
- —— Critical road network
- Local GDP increase
- **Nearest market**
  - Bottom 25%
  - Top 25%

Esri, HERE, DeLorme, Mapmyindia, © OpenStreetMap contributors, and the GIS user community

Estimated Deforestation: Forest Cover Loss

This section estimates the additional deforestation that may occur as a result of the major urban center road network improvement project. The process is similar to the above procedure for estimating incremental local GDP. In addition, the initial condition of the nearby road is used as a factor for simulating deforestation. Road condition is shown to be a significant determinant of deforestation in the analysis in chapter 3.

Map 4.3 shows current deforestation in the Democratic Republic of Congo for the period 2000–12, from Hansen and others (2013).[3] Deforestation in the country occurs for three main reasons: timber production (both formal and informal), wood fuel consumption, and land use change (mostly the conversion of forested

Map 4.3 Total Deforestation, 2000–12

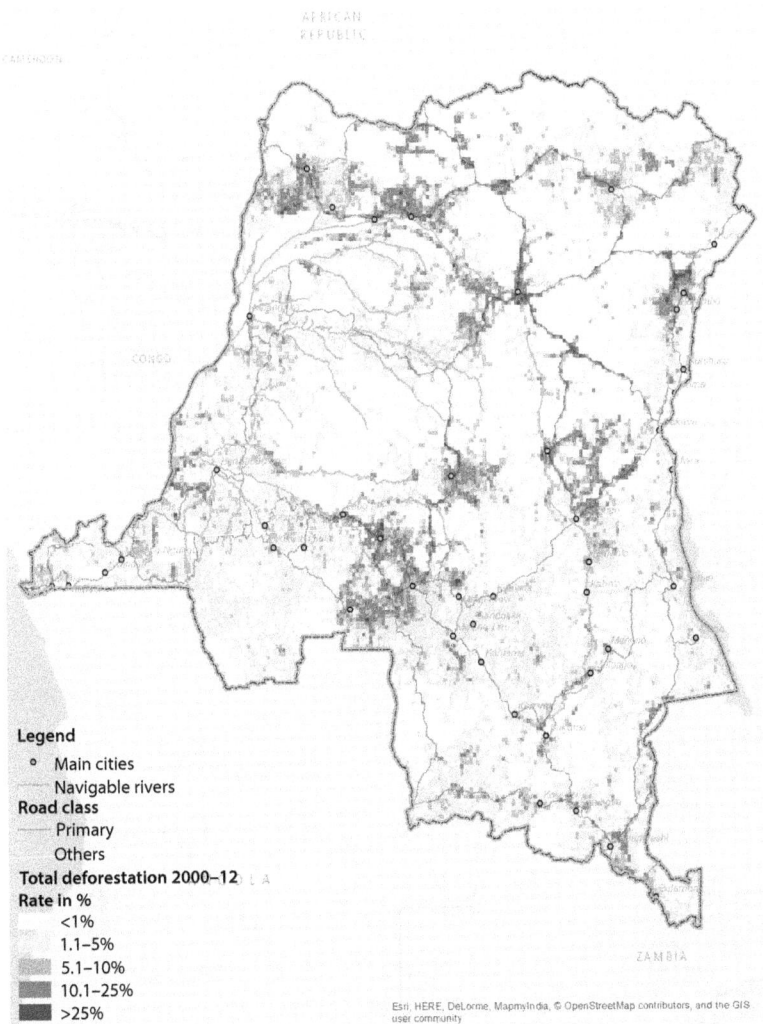

Legend
- ○ Main cities
- Navigable rivers

Road class
- Primary
- Others

Total deforestation 2000–12
Rate in %
- <1%
- 1.1–5%
- 5.1–10%
- 10.1–25%
- >25%

Esri, HERE, DeLorme, MapmyIndia, © OpenStreetMap contributors, and the GIS user community

Source: Hansen and others 2013.

areas into farmland). Despite insufficient data on how much deforestation is due to land conversion, it is clear that logging for wood fuel use outpaces timber production, with an estimated 72 million cubic meters of fuel wood consumed each year, relative to only 300,000 cubic meters of wood harvested in the formal timber sector, and an estimated 1.5 million to 2.4 million cubic meters of wood harvested in the informal timber sector annually (Debroux and others 2007).

As of 2016, the latest baseline forest cover provided by Landsat/TreeCover is for 2005 (Sexton and others 2013). Using Hansen and others' (2013) deforestation data, this Landsat data is then updated to reflect estimated tree cover for 2015, as shown in map 4.4.[4]

Map 4.4 Baseline Forest Cover, 2015

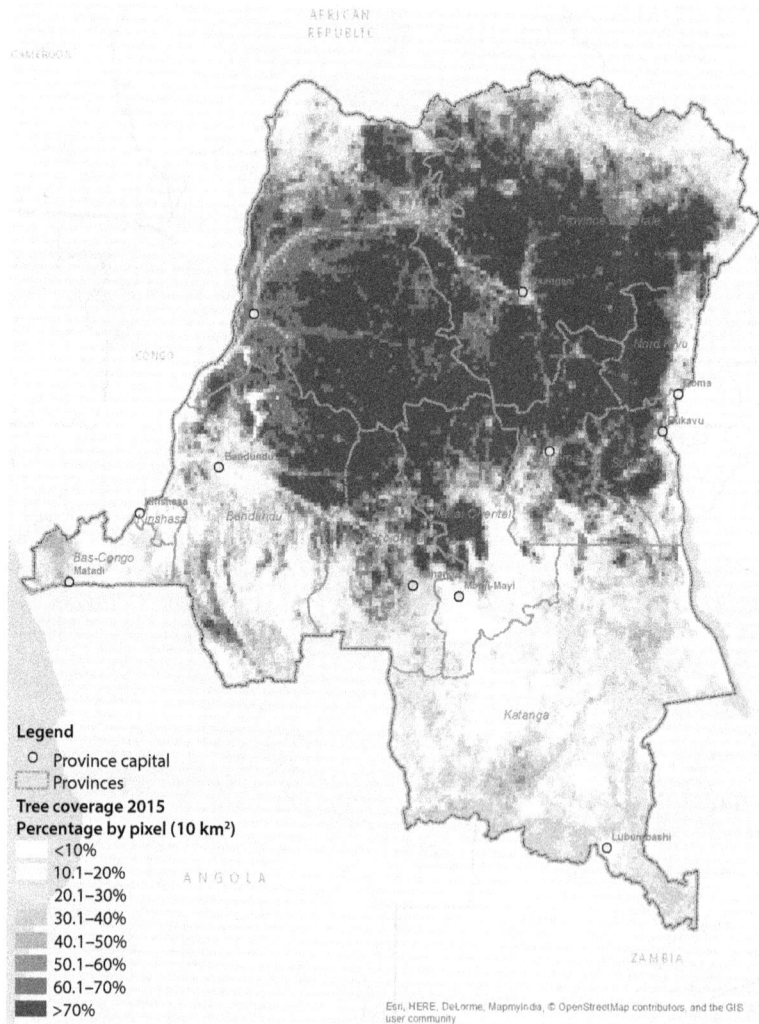

Source: Based on Hansen and others 2013.

Given the baseline 2015 tree cover data, and the elasticity of deforestation with respect to both transport cost reductions and road quality improvements, additional deforestation due to the major urban center road network project can now be estimated. The estimate is shown in map 4.5.[5] As the map shows, much of the additional deforestation will occur near the major cities of Kananga, Kisangani, and Maniema, as well as much of South Kivu and Maniema provinces.

Visualizing Opportunities and Safeguarding against Risks

This section combines the results from earlier in this chapter to examine the areas most affected, in both positive (higher local GDP) and negative

Map 4.5 Estimated Additional Deforestation from the Major Urban Center Road Network Improvement Project

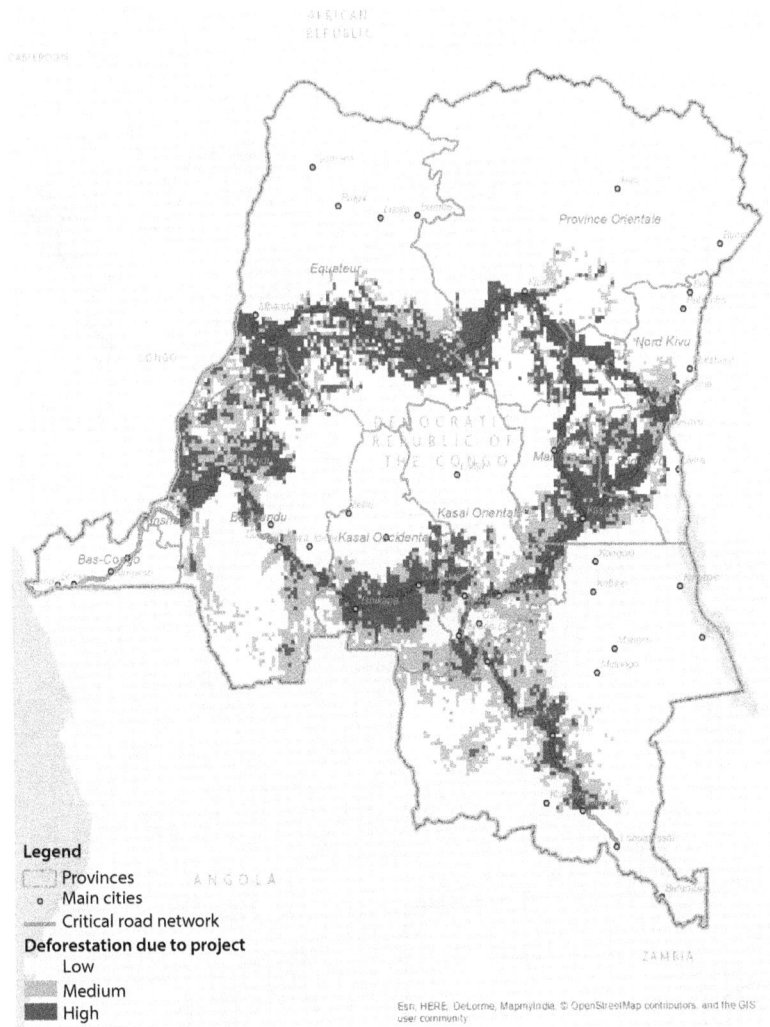

Legend
Provinces
○ Main cities
Critical road network
Deforestation due to project
Low
Medium
High

Esri, HERE, DeLorme, Mapmyindia, © OpenStreetMap contributors, and the GIS user community

Source: Based on Hansen and others 2013.

(increased deforestation and biodiversity loss) ways. However, before doing so, it is instructive to visualize the spatial distribution of the economy and ecology of the Democratic Republic of Congo. To do this, the intersection of local GDP (first presented in chapter 1, map 1.1), and the composite species-ecoregion index presented in chapter 3 (map 3.5), is shown in a combined map (map 4.6).

Map 4.6 shows that, quite often, the regions of the country that are most important economically also tend to contain the highest levels of sensitive biodiversity. The most important ecological areas, according to the composite species-ecoregion index, are along the eastern and southeastern borders of the country, the Congo River and its tributaries, and much of the provinces of

Map 4.6 The Economy and Ecology of the Democratic Republic of Congo

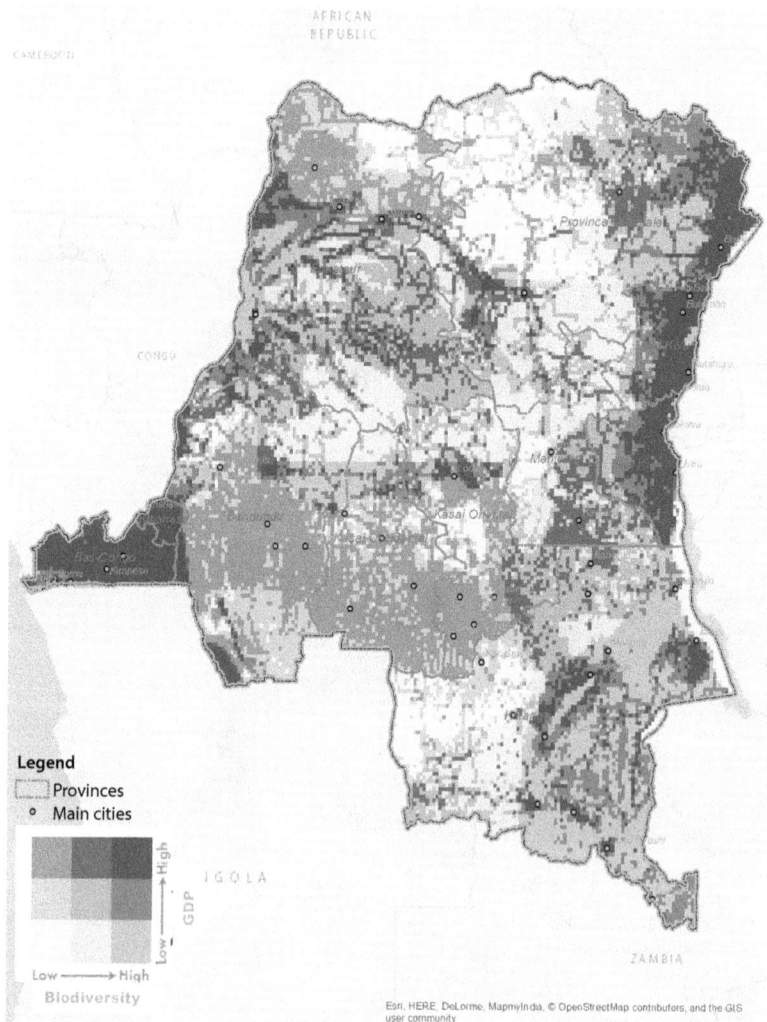

Source: Based on Ghosh and others 2010.

Bas Congo and Kinshasa. These also tend to be areas of higher population density and economic activity, with the notable exception of much of the eastern portion of Katanga province. Given that increased economic activity is typically followed by increased pressure on forests and biodiversity, significant risks from any development plan must be acknowledged so that effective policies and safeguards can be put in place.

To get a clearer picture of the economic and ecological impact of the major urban center road network improvement project, as a first step, changes in local GDP and deforestation are overlaid in one map to identify areas that would see the most benefits, or face the highest risks of loss.

- Areas in blue are "pure benefit" regions: local GDP gains are very significant, and deforestation increases are very low.
- Gold areas are the riskiest regions, and are estimated to have very low local GDP gains, but significant deforestation as a result of the project. These regions would benefit the most from being protected, given that there would be little economic activity lost, and there is a significant risk of deforestation.
- The intermediate zone is in gray.

Furthermore, as was shown by the composite species-ecoregion index, not all forested areas are equally important. To further prioritize the areas that would be most in need of protection, the regions at risk of the most deforestation are further dissected to reveal those that are most ecologically important. This task is accomplished by observing the intersection of the composite species-ecoregion index with the simulated deforestation due to the road improvement project. This result is shown in map 4.7. Note that the red, high-risk areas in map 4.7 are a subset of those in map 4.8. Given limited resources to put toward protection mechanisms, these red areas represent the regions most important to protect, while also having a low economic impact. The benefit of this exercise is that it shows that the truly high-risk areas appear to be small when threats from the road are considered. It also suggests where conservation efforts ought to be directed.

Virunga National Park Road Improvement Project

The same techniques are next used to examine the costs and benefits of a much smaller road improvement project, situated around Virunga National Park, shown in map 4.9. This project would improve a 525 kilometer road that connects the city of Goma, situated just south of Virunga National Park, between the park and Lake Kivu, to Bunia, approximately 100 kilometers north of the park, near Lake Albert. The pathway of the road is shown in map 4.9. Despite being a very populated area (approximately 4.5 million Congolese live within a small area around the road), the current condition of the road is quite poor, and in many areas, impassable. The 140 kilometer portion of the road that is paved is entirely in poor condition. The remaining 385 kilometers are unpaved, with 200 kilometers being in fair or good condition, and 185 kilometers in poor condition.

Map 4.7 Major Urban Center Road Network, High Ecological Risk Areas

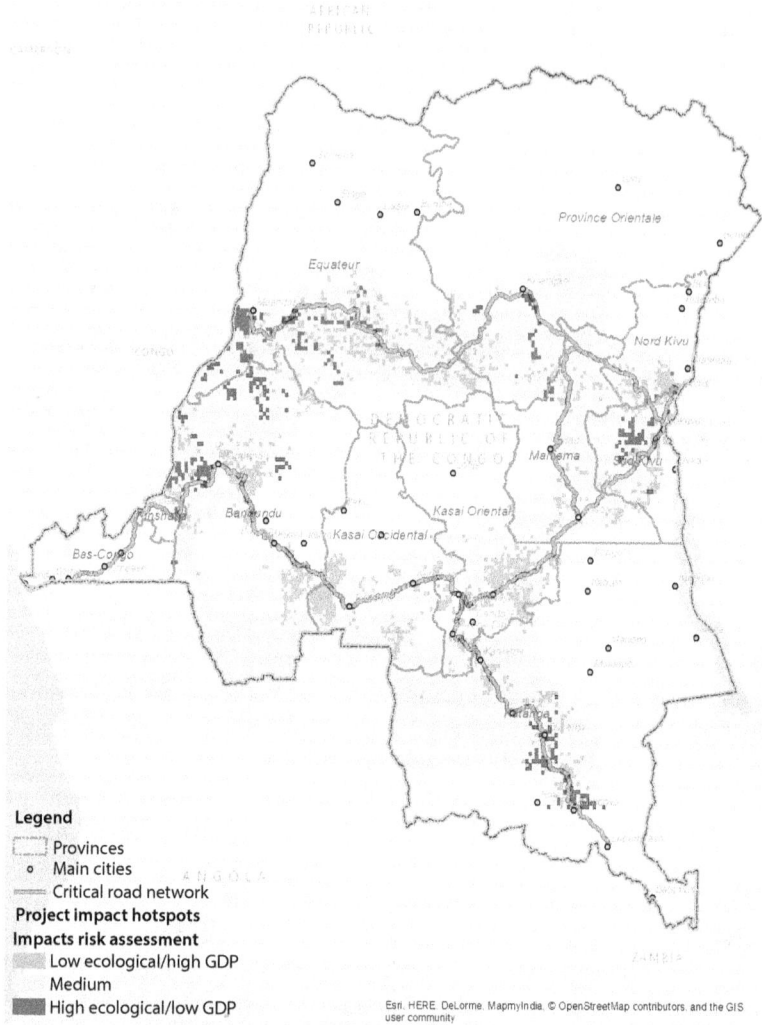

Legend
- ☐ Provinces
- ○ Main cities
- ═══ Critical road network

Project impact hotspots
Impacts risk assessment
- ▓ Low ecological/high GDP
- ▓ Medium
- ▓ High ecological/low GDP

Esri, HERE, DeLorme, MapmyIndia, © OpenStreetMap contributors, and the GIS user community

Sources: Based on Ghosh and others 2010 and Hansen and others 2013.

At first thought, improving this road may appear to offer a significant opportunity to spur economic growth in the region. The surrounding area has significant deposits of mineral wealth, including gold and the rare-earth mineral coltan. The land also contains very fertile soils with very high agricultural potential. Map 4.10 shows actual production yields versus potential yields for two important regional crops, cassava and bananas. The potential yields shown here are the "ideal agronomical potential," that is, the yields that could be obtained given a very high level of inputs and laboratory-like conditions. Although these conditions could, of course, never be achieved, these images clearly show that there is significant room for yield improvement, and improving market access for farmers in the region may provide both the means and the incentives to adopt more

Map 4.8 Major Urban Center Road Network Deforestation Risk Assessment

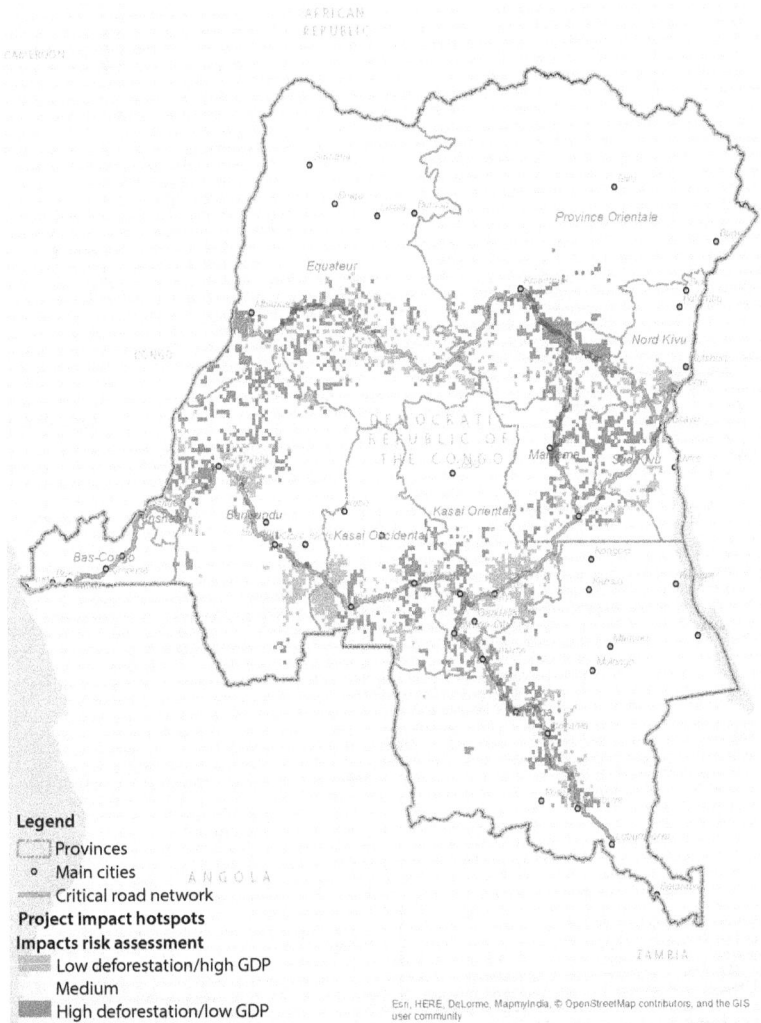

Legend
- Provinces
- ○ Main cities
- Critical road network
- **Project impact hotspots**
- **Impacts risk assessment**
  - Low deforestation/high GDP
  - Medium
  - High deforestation/low GDP

Esri, HERE, DeLorme, Mapmyindia, © OpenStreetMap contributors, and the GIS user community

Sources: Based on Ghosh and others 2010 and Hansen and others 2013.

input-intensive farming techniques to improve yields (see box 4.2 for a discussion on estimating agricultural benefits of the Virunga National Park road improvement project). Without taking into consideration any externalities, this road appears to be a major candidate for significant investments to spur economic activity.

Nevertheless, road infrastructure development in this region may come with deep trade-offs. The land around the potential road project is heavily forested and includes one of the world's most important national parks. Virunga National Park was established in 1924 and was the first designated national park in Africa. Originally established to protect one of only two

Map 4.9 Virunga National Park Road Improvement Map

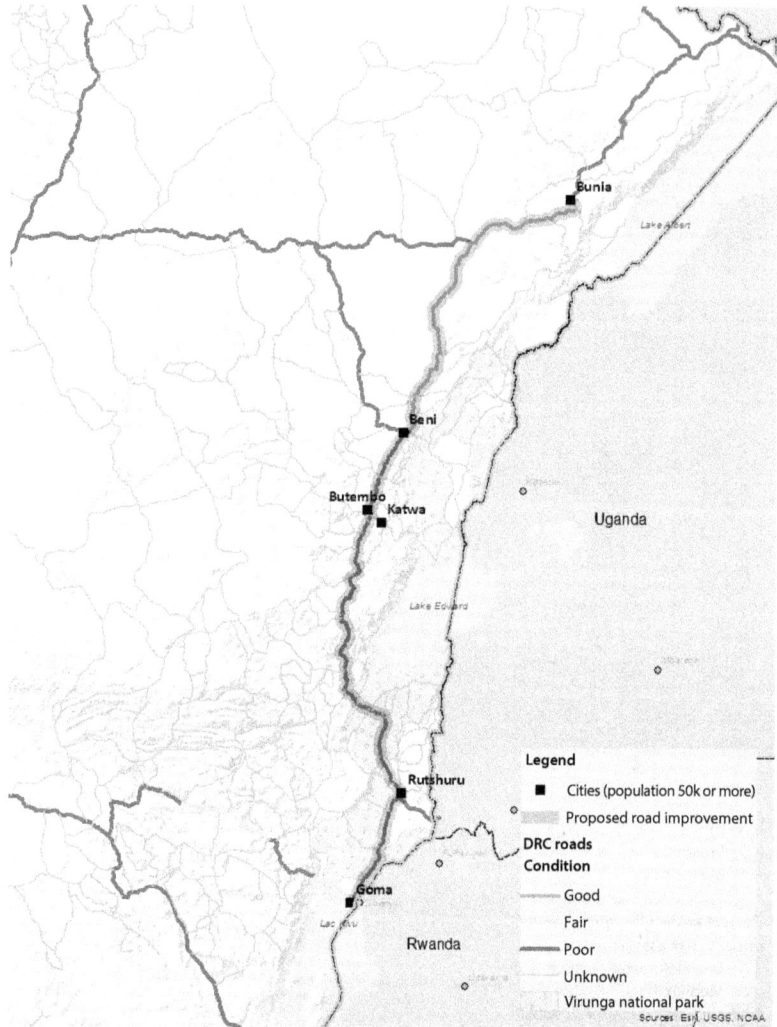

Source: Based on Africa Infrastructure Country Diagnostics, http://infrastructureafrica.org/.

populations in the world of the now critically endangered mountain gorilla, the park also contains other exceptional biodiversity, including both the forest and savannah elephants, okapi, giraffes, and chimpanzees. As demonstrated in chapter 3, improving the road around Virunga could potentially disrupt this biome. Environmental factors aside, Virunga National Park could become one of the greatest tourist attractions on the continent if the conflict and security issues in the eastern part of the country could be resolved. Destroying this natural capital would therefore not only be an environmental tragedy, but would also eliminate a potentially significant source of future income for the country's impoverished inhabitants.

Map 4.10 Actual Production Yields versus Potential Yields for Cassava and Banana

a. Actual cassava yields

b. Potential cassava yields

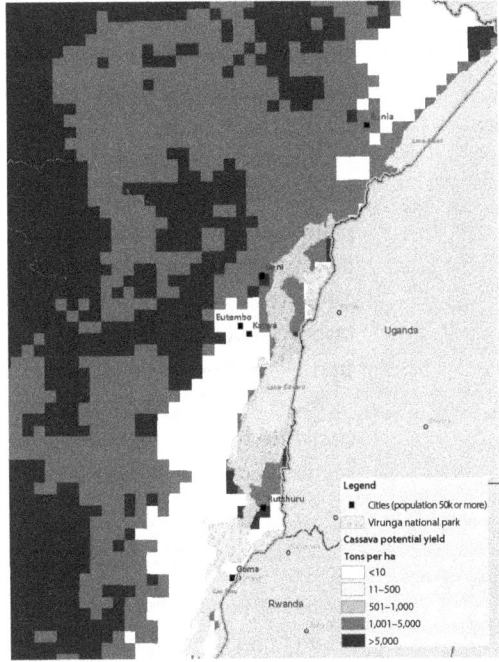

c. Actual banana yields

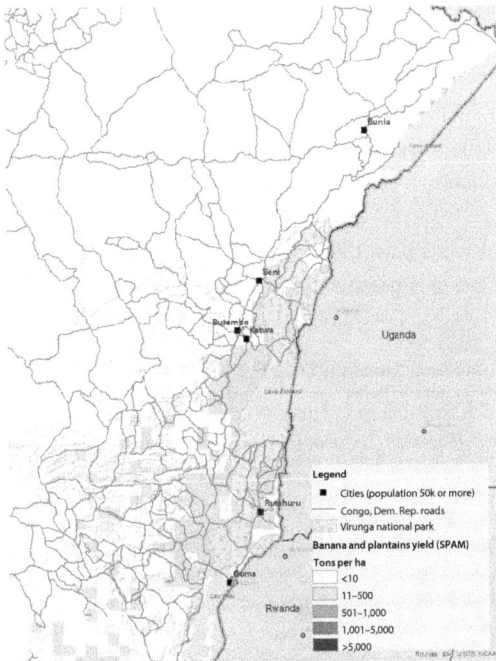

d. Potential banana yields

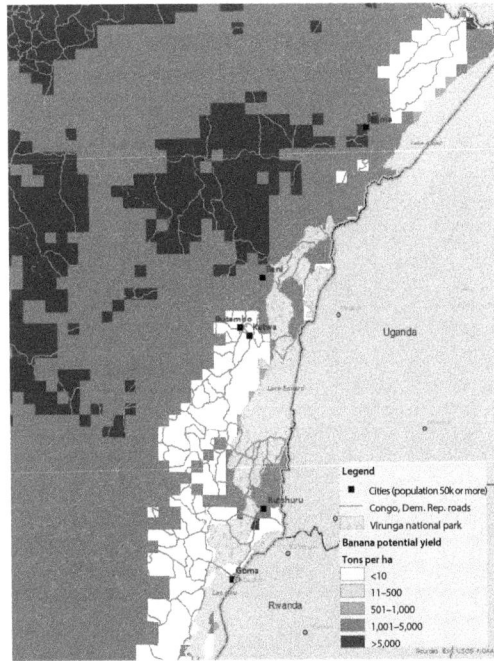

Sources: Actual production yields are in tons per hectare and are from the Spatial Production Allocation Model from HarvestChoice (2012) for 2000. Potential yields are also in tons per hectare and are from FAO and IIASA (2000), and depend on soil and climate conditions.

Box 4.2 Estimating Agricultural Benefits

This report focuses on estimating aggregate, multisector economic benefits from road construction. However, a similar methodology can be used to estimate benefits for a particular sector. The only requirements are spatially disaggregated output data and a production function that holds under the assumptions of linear econometric estimation strategies. Estimating an agricultural production function is quite common in the economics literature, and for the Democratic Republic of Congo requires very little additional data. Because most agricultural production is at the subsistence level, it is safe to assume that the only major inputs are land (for example, soil quality and climate) and labor (for which population in the surrounding area can serve as a proxy). In addition, a novel data set known as the Spatial Production Allocation Model (SPAM) from HarvestChoice (2012) provides baseline agricultural production data, by crop, in a gridded fashion similar to the presentation of local GDP data in this study.

Using the SPAM data, an agricultural production function can be estimated that generates elasticities describing how production of a given crop changes for a percentage change in market transport costs. This agricultural production function is given by the following equation:

$$\ln\left(P_i^k\right) = \beta_0 + \beta_1 \ln(TM_i) + X_i'\gamma + \varepsilon_i, \tag{B4.2.1}$$

in which P_i^k denotes the total production of crop k in grid cell i, TM_i is the transport cost to market, and X_i is a vector of regional controls. Those controls include ln(population), ln(population)^2, ln(crop k potential yield), ln(crop k potential yield)^2, ln(distance to nearest mine), and a measure of conflict near the grid cell and the local market. As with the local GDP regressions, to account for the endogeneity of both market cost and the conflict variables, this calculation takes an instrumental variable approach following Ali (2015) (see Ali and others [2015] for details on the instrumental variables used and a discussion of the conflict measures).

With each crop estimated separately, national crop-specific elasticities are calculated. Those elasticities are shown in table B4.2.1. Note that the elasticities are modified so that they show the percentage change in crop production for a corresponding 10 percent reduction in market transport costs.

The results show that bananas and plantains have the highest transport cost elasticities, which is not surprising given that they are highly perishable and therefore need to be sold

Table B4.2.1 Impact of Transport Cost Reductions on Crop Production

Crop	Elasticity (percent change in crop production for each 10 percent reduction in market transport costs)
Cassava	2.6***
Bananas or plantains	12.4***
Maize	0.11
Ground nuts	6.6***
Rice	4.6***
Beans	12.3***

Significance level: *** = 1 percent.

box continues next page

quickly after harvesting. In contrast, cassava and rice, which are highly nonperishable, have relatively low transport cost elasticity, reflecting the fact that market access may not be such an important factor when it comes to production decisions.

Using these elasticities, simulations on agricultural output performed similarly to the simulations on local GDP in this report would be straightforward. Note that because the data are at the spatially gridded level, and not the farmer or plot level, the simulation results would be agnostic with respect to whether the production change is caused by intensification (improving yields on a given plot of land) or extensification (increasing the amount of land under cultivation). However, a more complex model that also takes into account total harvested area could be adopted to distinguish between these two mechanisms.

The immense trade-offs that accompany this project make it a fitting example of a project that would benefit from the analysis developed in this report. The next two subsections show the calculations needed to quantitatively evaluate the costs and benefits of this project.

Estimated Benefits: Increase in Local GDP

As with the major urban center road network simulation, this simulation begins with an estimate of local transport costs to the cheapest market. First, the optimal route and the transport cost associated with that route are calculated, given the current condition of the road segment. The geospatial model is then updated to reflect the entirety of this road being upgraded to good condition. Map 4.11 shows the original transport costs before the improvement, and the estimated reduction in transport costs due to the intervention. As would be expected, transport costs are lowest nearest to the road and the major cities (which are also markets according to the definition in the geospatial model), and increase with a fairly even gradient as one moves away from the main population center around the border with Rwanda and Uganda. Similarly, the bulk of the transport cost reduction occurs for those living close to the road because the reduction is measured as a percentage of the original transport cost. Individuals living farther from the road being improved will spend less time using the improved road, so their overall transport costs are reduced by a lower percentage, even if the overall level of transport costs declines more.

Next, local elasticities are generated using the methodology described in chapter 2. Benefits—the increase in local GDP—are then calculated at the grid cell level (approximate 10 kilometers ×10 kilometers), and aggregated to arrive at a final range of US$7.29 million–US$31.9 million per year above the baseline, depending on whether local elasticities or the national elasticity (calculated in box 2.2 of chapter 2) is used. Map 4.12 shows the distribution of these benefits. Note that they are even more clustered around the road than are the changes in transport costs, shown in map 4.11. This outcome occurs because the increase in local GDP is a function that increases with both the baseline local GDP and

Map 4.11 Virunga National Park Regional Transport Cost before and after the Intervention

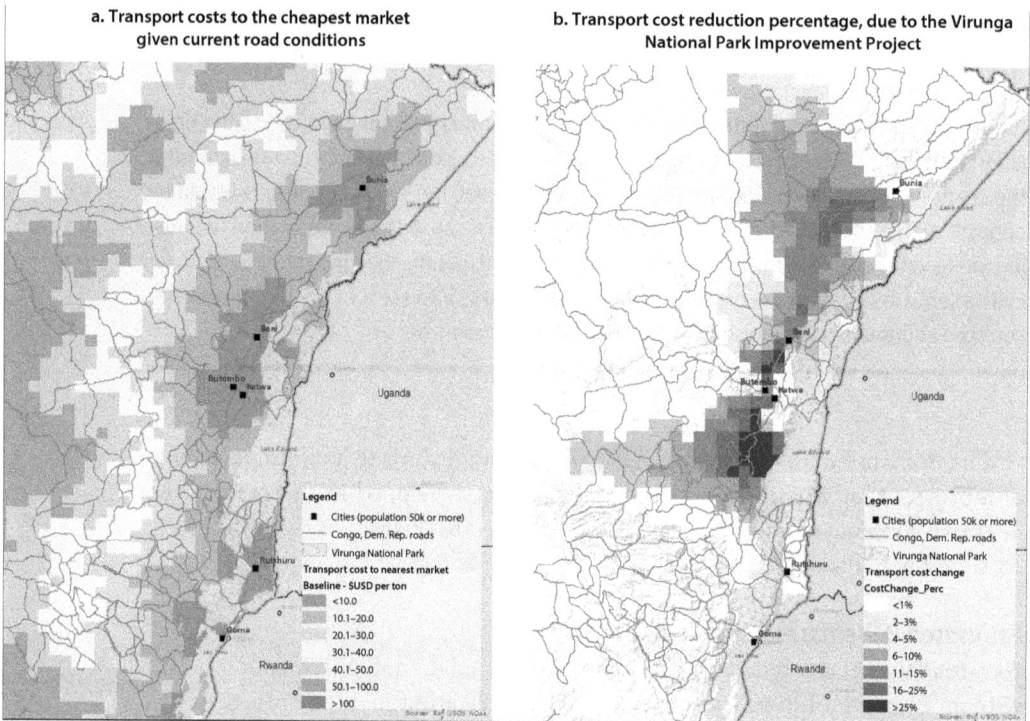

a. Transport costs to the cheapest market given current road conditions

b. Transport cost reduction percentage, due to the Virunga National Park Improvement Project

the percentage reduction in transport costs, both of which are highly clustered around the road. Multiplying these two magnifies this clustering even further. Again, several caveats must be noted. First, it is unlikely that these benefits would occur all at once. Rather, the benefits would likely layer in over several years as individuals in this region adapt to the new infrastructure, make new investments in their farms or business, and set up new networks in the cities in the region. Second, this methodology only estimates the benefits to an increase in *local* transport to the cheapest market. Having cheaper access to multiple markets may bring additional benefits. Finally, these are gross benefits and factor in neither the cost of the road upgrade nor ongoing maintenance costs.

Estimated Deforestation: Forest Cover Loss

Using the methodology established in chapter 3, the predicted additional deforestation due to the Virunga National Park road improvement project is now estimated to see which regions are most at risk. Baseline forest cover in 2012 is shown in map 4.13. As is evident from the map, considerable deforestation has already occurred around the region of the road.

Map 4.14 now shows the estimated annual new deforestation that would occur due to the road improvement project. The biggest risk of deforestation is to those regions that have already shown a propensity to be deforested, and that

Map 4.12 Local GDP Change due to the Virunga National Park Road Improvement Project

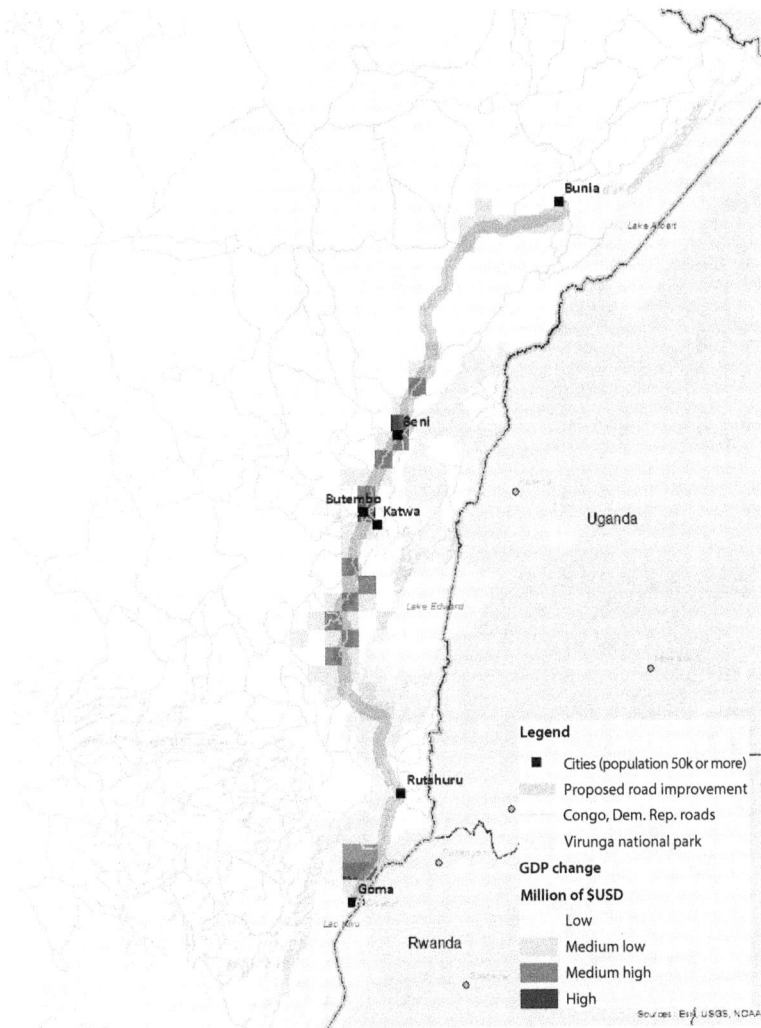

Source: Baseline local GDP is from Ghosh and others 2010.
Note: GDP increase is shown in qualitative terms because the actual values are dependent on the elasticity chosen for the simulation. Because all cells are multiplied by the same elasticity, choosing the locally estimated elasticity instead of the national elasticity will result in the same percentage change in local GDP for every cell, and therefore the relative difference in local GDP will remain the same, as shown in the map.

are nearest to the population centers and the improved road. This simulation shows that the areas that would be most stressed are near Lake Edward, the corridor between Goma and Rutshuru, and the corridor from Katwa to Butembo to Beni. To a much lesser extent, additional deforestation may also occur to the west and northwest of Bunia and to the northwest of Goma.

As a final step in the analysis, the estimated additional deforestation due to the project is layered on top of the current biodiversity index to see which

Map 4.13 Baseline Forest Cover, 2012, Virunga National Park

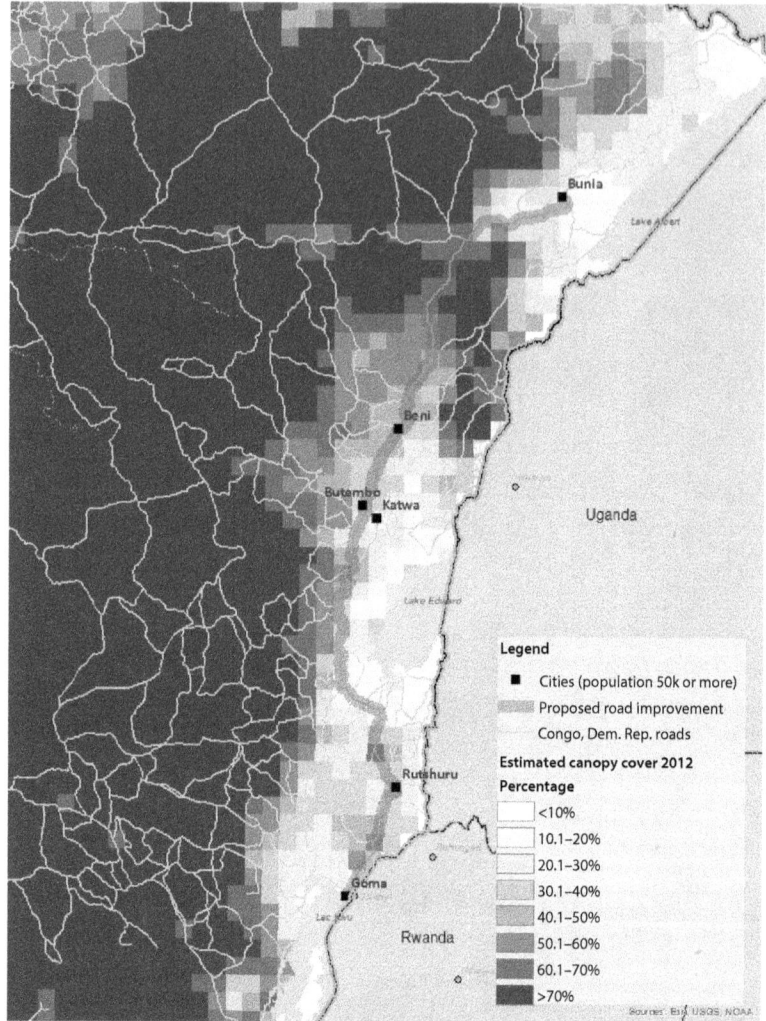

Source: Based on Hansen and others 2013.

threatened areas have the most biodiversity, and are therefore most worth protecting. This composite is shown in map 4.15. The grid cells outlined in black are those in which deforestation is predicted to increase because of the project. Although the intensity of deforestation is not measured, the map allows the gradient of biodiversity within the affected areas to be compared to discern which areas are ecologically most important. Comparing map 4.14 with map 4.15, it is clear that some of the regions with the highest ecological value also coincide with the regions predicted to experience the highest rate of deforestation from the project.

Map 4.14 Additional Annual Deforestation due to the Virunga National Park Road Improvement Project

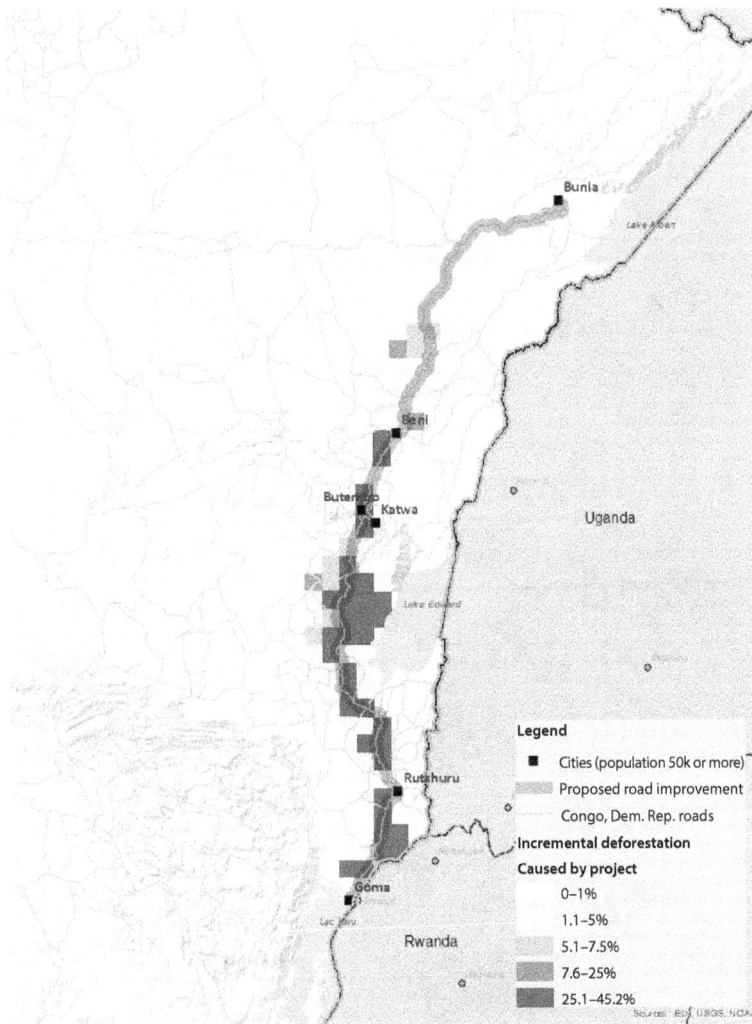

Source: Based on Hansen and others 2013.

The important conclusion is that the Virunga National Park road project poses a very significant risk to the forests and to high-value biodiversity in the region. Before undertaking such a project, stakeholders should carefully compare the estimated benefits with these costs to ensure the trade-offs are worthwhile. This analysis also identifies the regions most at risk, so that if the project is deemed to be economically viable, safeguards can be put in place to protect the most fragile and vulnerable areas.

Map 4.15 Biodiversity Composite Index Compared with Estimated Additional Deforestation due to the Project

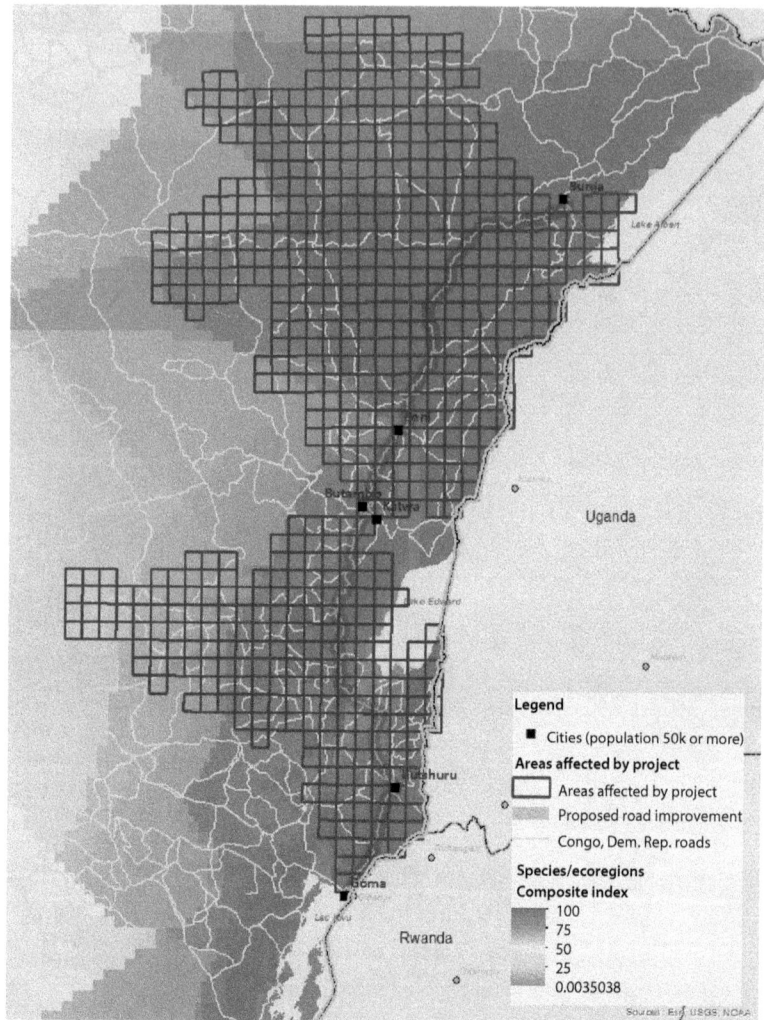

Notes

1. That is, using the newly upgraded network, the optimal route to the cheapest market is reestimated following the same procedure, thereby obtaining the cheapest travel cost for every cell, under the scenario that each of these roads is entirely in good condition. Then the results are compared with the baseline scenario to obtain the change in transport costs for each grid cell due to the project. Note that the spatial model uses tertiary, secondary, and primary roads, thereby capturing rural connectivity and market issues at the same time.

2. This image looks remarkably similar to map 4.1, which is to be expected; the difference between them is that the data used to create map 4.2 are multiplied by local GDP and the local GDP elasticity to transport costs.

3. Trees are defined as vegetation taller than five meters and are expressed as a percentage per output grid cell. "Forest cover loss" is defined as a stand-replacement disturbance, or a change from a forest to nonforest state, during the period.

4. Deforestation data are available from 2000 to 2012 (Hansen and others 2013). It is assumed that the average deforestation rate in each 10 square kilometer cell continues for 2013 and 2014 to arrive at the 2015 tree cover map.

5. To calculate this, the annual average number of pixels lost to deforestation in the recent past (2000–12), the change in transport costs (to the local market) due to the project, and the elasticities of number of pixels cleared to changes in transport costs (see chapter 3 for an explanation of this elasticity) were all used to simulate the effect of improving the road and reducing the transport cost to the local market.

References

Ali, R., A. F. Barra, C. N. Berg, R. Damania, J. D. Nash, and J. Russ. 2015. "Infrastructure in Conflict-Prone and Fragile Environments: Evidence from the Democratic Republic of Congo." Policy Research Working Paper 7273, World Bank, Washington, DC.

Debroux, Laurent, T. Hart, D. Kaimowitz, A. Karsenty, and G. Topa, eds. 2007. *Forests in Post-Conflict Democratic Republic of Congo: Analysis of a Priority Agenda*. Jakarta: Center for International Forestry Research.

FAO and IIASA (Food and Agricultural Organization of the United Nations and International Institute for Applied Systems Analysis). 2000. *Global Agro-Ecological Zones (GAEZ)*.

Ghosh, T., R. L. Powell, C. D. Elvidge, K. E. Baugh, P. C. Sutton, and S. Anderson. 2010. "Shedding Light on the Global Distribution of Economic Activity." *Open Geography Journal* 3 (1): 148–61.

Hansen, M. C., P. V. Potapov, R. Moore, M. Hancher, S. A. Turubanova, A. Tyukavina, D. Thau, S. V. Stehman, S. J. Goetz, T. R. Loveland, A. Kommareddy, A. Egorov, L. Chini, C. O. Justice, and J. R. G. Townshend. 2013. "High-Resolution Global Maps of 21st-Century Forest Cover Change." *Science* 342 (6160): 850–53.

HarvestChoice. 2012. *Spatial Allocation of Agricultural Production*. Washington, DC: International Food Policy Research Institute. http://harvestchoice.org/node/2248.

Sexton, J. O., X.-P. Song, M. Feng, P. Noojipady, A. Anand, C. Huang, D.-H. Kim, K. M. Collins, S. Channan, C. DiMiceli, and J. R. G. Townshend. 2013. "Global, 30-m Resolution Continuous Fields of Tree Cover: Landsat-Based Rescaling of MODIS Vegetation Continuous Fields with Lidar-Based Estimates of Error." *International Journal of Digital Earth* 6 (5): 427–48. doi:10.1080/17538947.2013.786146.

CHAPTER 5

Summary and Conclusions

Introduction

The Democratic Republic of Congo's transport infrastructure is among the sparsest and most dilapidated in the world. Although improving the transport network will not be sufficient to cause growth and raise the millions of Congolese out of extreme poverty, any successful development plan must include infrastructure investment as a core component. The purpose of this study is therefore to demonstrate several techniques that can be used to evaluate pathways to sustainable growth in the country via transportation infrastructure improvement. This report attempts to take a holistic approach to evaluating the impact of road network improvement. Chapter 2 provides an overview of the current state of the Democratic Republic of Congo's transport system, prescribes two potential transport investment opportunities, and presents an econometric model for estimating the economic benefits from reducing local transportation costs. Chapter 3 examines the potential deforestation that could occur from infrastructure investments, specifically estimating total losses as well as possible biodiversity impacts on the local biome. Finally, chapter 4 combines the knowledge from the previous chapters to simulate the effects of improving a national roads network that connects major urban centers with Kinshasa, as well as of improving a local road near Virunga National Park. The report estimates both economic benefits due to local transport cost reductions and costs in the form of additional forest depletion.

Modeling Transport Cost in the Democratic Republic of Congo and Its Effects in the Economy

A geospatial model was developed to simulate how individuals and traded goods are moved around the country. This model takes the road and river network (including both location and quality information), land topography, and population data as inputs, and makes several simplifying, yet plausible assumptions about how local farmers, traders, and other economic agents will move around the country. The culmination is a model that can be used to estimate transport costs to and from any location within the Democratic Republic of Congo, that is, transport routes that a cost minimizer would take to ship products to market.

From the analysis it is clear that, aside from some isolated areas in the northwest part of the country, rivers are used relatively infrequently for local transport. Specifically, only 14 percent of individuals and 7 percent of the country's gross domestic product (GDP) are in areas where it would be cost-effective to use river transport for any portion of the trip to the local market. Thus, investments in river transport will not have a significant impact on local market transport, given the current economic geography of the country. It is therefore evident that the road network is likely to be much more important for local transport than are rivers. However, access to river transport becomes more important for longer-distance travel and for goods with a relatively low value-to-bulk ratio. When minimizing travel costs to Kinshasa, the geospatial model indicates that approximately 80 percent of the Democratic Republic of Congo's population, and nearly 60 percent of GDP, are in areas where the more efficient travel path uses river travel, at least in part, to transport goods to Kinshasa. Although cost savings to local transport are quite low and confined to areas right along the river, cost savings for transport to Kinshasa are much greater and spread throughout most of the country, save the southern part, which is mostly outside of the Congo Basin.

Finally, an econometric model is estimated that shows how reducing transport costs to the local market can have an impact on GDP. When controlling for various important factors, including local population, agricultural land quality, proximity to mining sites, and the presence of conflict, it is found that reducing transport costs by 10 percent can, on average, increase local GDP by 0.46 percent. Although it may be intuitive that reducing transport costs can have a positive impact on the economy, quantifying these benefits is useful for conducting impact analyses, as is demonstrated in chapter 4.

Estimating Deforestation and Biodiversity Impacts of Road Improvements

Using the best available data and robust econometric techniques, the report also finds large and highly significant effects of road upgrading on the intensity and extent of forest clearing in road corridors. Predicted effects of deforestation around improved road corridors vary widely with previous road conditions and locational economics, but increases in deforestation of 10–20 percent are typical. More specifically, the deforestation assessment finds remarkably robust and stable econometric estimates across different statistical specifications in the regressions, suggesting that forest clearing intensity declines on average with distance from roads, proximity to protected areas, and less accessible terrain (for example, higher elevation). It increases on average with improvements in road conditions, the agricultural value of land (opportunity cost), proximity to population agglomerations (that is, urban centers), and conflict intensity. Two patterns are noteworthy. First, upgrading roads from very poor to good condition produces near-complete deforestation within a narrow corridor (a radius of about 1–1.5 kilometers) straddling the road. Second, the impact is nonlinear, and deforestation intensity falls very rapidly as distance from the road increases. Most of the deforestation occurs within about a 2 kilometer radius of the road.

Because not all forest land is of uniform ecological value, nor is it of uniform economic value, this report also develops a metric for identifying areas that are both of high ecological value and at higher risk of degradation. A high-resolution map of ecological vulnerability is developed that combines information on species as well as ecosystems, including measures of geographic vulnerability, extinction risk, and other aspects of the ecosystem captured through a measure of biomes developed by the World Wildlife Fund.

Overall, the results suggest that the siting process for infrastructure needs to consider effects on deforestation and biodiversity loss at the very outset of planning. Sequential decision making whereby the location decision occurs first, followed by an environmental impact assessment, can lead to economically less favorable outcomes that can be avoided through careful upstream planning.

Scenario Analysis

In the final chapter, the econometric results from chapters 2 and 3 are used in two simulations to estimate the potential welfare benefits, as well as deforestation, that would result from the implementation of (1) a proposed road investment project that connects major urban centers to Kinshasa with high-quality roads in good condition, and (2) a road connecting two major cities in the eastern part of the country. Keeping in mind that the benefits are estimated using a partial equilibrium framework, and that the benefits are only a subset of the total benefits from reducing transport costs (other benefits include those stemming from improved transport between cities, increased access to multiple cities rather than solely the cheapest one, and better access to ports), these estimates are likely a very conservative, minimum benefit.

In a similar manner, simulations are used to estimate the total extent of deforestation attributable to these two projects. The methodology identifies areas that are most at risk for new deforestation resulting from the project. It also allows for areas of high ecological value to be prioritized by overlaying a composite biodiversity index, which accounts for the fact that not all forests are identical and the ecological value of different regions can vary significantly.

Finally, the results from the major urban center road network project are combined to create a map that provides an indication of which areas of the country would benefit most from the proposed project, and which areas would suffer the greatest risks from deforestation. Maps similar to these can be used to help plan the location of future transportation investment projects and help ensure these projects have the largest expected economic benefits, while also minimizing environmental impacts.

It is important to conclude by highlighting the caveats to this analysis. First, the assessment has been conducted in an environment in which data are limited, so there would be merit in replicating the analysis with better data. Second, no attempt has been made to conduct a full cost-benefit analysis. This omission partly reflects the difficulties in defining environmental costs and benefits, especially those related to biodiversity. Third, the simulations are based on the assumption that all benefits are immediate; in reality, benefits would evolve as the economy moves to a new equilibrium. Fourth, because the analysis is dealing with aggregate benefits, it is unable to identify which sectors of the economy would be most responsive to transport cost improvements, or would be most likely to result in environmental damage. Once more, this shortcoming reflects the lack of data at the desired spatial scale. Finally, the focus of the report is on benefits that derive from reductions in transport costs to local markets. Extending the analysis to other markets or complementing the estimates with those derived from gravity models of interregional trade would be straightforward processes.

Environmental Benefits Statement

The World Bank Group is committed to reducing its environmental footprint. In support of this commitment, the Publishing and Knowledge Division leverages electronic publishing options and print-on-demand technology, which is located in regional hubs worldwide. Together, these initiatives enable print runs to be lowered and shipping distances decreased, resulting in reduced paper consumption, chemical use, greenhouse gas emissions, and waste.

The Publishing and Knowledge Division follows the recommended standards for paper use set by the Green Press Initiative. The majority of our books are printed on Forest Stewardship Council (FSC)–certified paper, with nearly all containing 50–100 percent recycled content. The recycled fiber in our book paper is either unbleached or bleached using totally chlorine-free (TCF), processed chlorine-free (PCF), or enhanced elemental chlorine-free (EECF) processes.

More information about the Bank's environmental philosophy can be found at http://www.worldbank.org/corporateresponsibility.

green press INITIATIVE

www.ingramcontent.com/pod-product-compliance
Lightning Source LLC
Chambersburg PA
CBHW080001280326
41935CB00013B/1715